FOLLOWING
THE
RED BIRD

First steps into a life of faith

KATE H. RADEMACHER

Light M

Durham, NC

Published 2017 by Light Messages Publishing
www.lightmessages.com
Durham, NC 27713 USA
SAN: 920-9298

Paperback ISBN: 978-1-61153-223-4
E-book ISBN: 978-1-61153-222-7
Library of Congress Control Number: 2017931514

To David
for all the ways you inspire and support me
and
to Soren and Lila

They were all still wondering what to do next, when Lucy said, "Look! There's a robin, with such a red breast. It's the first bird I've seen here. I say!—I wonder can birds talk in Narnia? It almost looks as if it wanted to say something to us." Then she turned to the Robin and said, "Please, can you tell us where Tumnus the Faun has been taken to?" As she said this she took a step toward the bird. It at once flew away but only as far as to the next tree. There it perched and looked at them very hard as if it understood all they had been saying. Almost without noticing that they had done so, the four children went a step or two nearer to it. At this the Robin flew away again to the next tree and once more looked at them very hard. (You couldn't have found a robin with a redder chest or a brighter eye.) "Do you know," said Lucy, "I really believe he means us to follow him."

–C.S. Lewis, *The Lion, the Witch and the Wardrobe*

INTRODUCTION

SURROUNDED BY THREE HUNDRED parishioners, I sat in the front pew of the church, barefoot and in a long, floor-length white robe. It was the night before Easter. In twenty minutes I would be baptized by full immersion, and I was twitching in my seat uncomfortably. It wasn't because I was having last-minute doubts, like a bride hoping for someone to chime in on the, "Speak now or forever hold your peace." Nor was it because I was wondering how I'd gotten there—how a liberal, secular skeptic in her mid-thirties ends up loving God with her whole heart. No, it was much more mundane. I'd had about five glasses of water at dinner, and now I really had to go to the bathroom. The Great Vigil before Easter is an extremely long service.

If you've ever sat in the first row in church and had to sneak out to go to the bathroom, then you are familiar with the ordinary awkwardness of scurrying off between hymns in a half crouch. But the intense social discomfort

I

of getting up from the front pew during a service is like no other when you have two priests, three baptismal sponsors, a lapsed Episcopalian turned Unitarian Universalist mother, a lapsed agnostic turned Catholic father, a Buddhist husband, a Baptist brother, an atheist brother, two Mormon cousins, and about ten friends all gathered to watch you get reborn as a child of Christ. I was worried that they might think I was heading for my get-away car. Yet I had to make the tough choice to get up and cross, barefoot and robed, in front of the altar and all those people—the only option for a quick exit. The alternative was to risk peeing in the baptismal font.

This book is about tough choices. It is about the tough choice to treat the voice of the divine, which I hear as a striking and distinct whisper in my heart, as something that is real. The tough choice to let myself fall head over heels in love with Christianity, despite the derision with which it is treated in most of my circles. The choice to let God's love in, and to realize that God was ready and wanting me to start down a new path to get closer to Him. Most of all, it's about the choice to start to surrender my own squirrely, self-interested ways and follow God's lead, turning back again and again in an earnest attempt to discern and honor God's will.

This book is also about choosing to respond to an unexpected and voracious vocational calling. Just a few weeks after I was baptized, I felt a restless impulse to begin writing about my spiritual journey. I got in the car one day, intending to head to a coffee shop with my laptop to jot down some thoughts. Instead, I felt a strong intuition to head to the local bookstore; the car practically drove itself there. After arriving, I experienced a nudge to pick up T.M. Luhrmann's book, *When God Talks Back*. In this four-hundred-page tome, Luhrmann, an anthropologist, explains how some Christians experience God. I felt a deep shock of being seen and known within these pages. This author describes a way of listening for and experiencing God's voice that matched my experience almost perfectly. After observing and interviewing hundreds of Christians, Luhrmann wrote, "What I saw was that coming to a committed belief in God was more like learning to *do* something than to think something…. The way you learn to pay attention determines your experience of God…. In effect, people train the mind in such a way that they experience part of their mind as the presence of God…"

Reading this was startling. It described exactly how I had come to experience God over the past three years as an external presence that manifested as an internal experience within my mind. For me, knowing God in this way did not initially emerge from following any formal instructions. Rather, it evolved slowly by following the breadcrumbs the Spirit seemed to leave out—one by one—as I came to know God as a living presence in my life. I was like the children in C.S. Lewis' beloved novel, following the red bird through the woods in Narnia, one step at a time as it flitted from branch to branch, leading them forward through unfamiliar territory.

At the same time, however, I wanted more structured guidance. I found that few Christian books talk about the mechanics of how listening for and hearing God's voice actually *works*. I wanted more of a how-to manual. And so, in a small way, this book responds to that need. Although not actually a how-to manual, I do attempt to provide concrete examples of how I've come to hear God: as an internal presence that is distinct from my own restless mind; in the small, Spirit-filled nudges here and there like the one I felt at the bookstore; through imaginative prayer; through the practice of sacred reading called *lectio divina*; and through assuming an inner attitude of surrender once I've gotten even a foggy sense of what God's calling me to do.

These ways of deeply listening and responding to the inner voice of God—including feeling the presence of Jesus—have had overtly political and social implications in my life. Most notably, I feel that God both affirms and shapes my professional work in public health which focuses on helping increase access to contraception around the world. I truly feel that in my prayers, God has told me that my calling is to help promote birth control. Yet, with contraception remaining a controversial subject in the American political and religious landscape, I can imagine some questioning the authenticity of this claim—that God *really* called me to this work rather than my perception being folly or ego-driven distortion. During this journey, I have come to recognize that it is very possible—even probable—that God has told another person down the street that it is her calling to work *against* birth control. This story includes how I have come to believe that there may be true spiritual integrity in the prayerful guidance that others have received which contradicts my own calling. I see that perhaps God has given us this creative tension so that we can work together to work it out so that we can eventually do God's will "on earth as it is in heaven."

On the day of my baptism, I scurried back from the bathroom, picking up my robes to avoid the added embarrassment of tripping headlong in front of the altar, and settled back into my pew. My six-year-old daughter meanwhile had slid to the floor and was lying under the seat where she was playing with a toy we had brought to keep her entertained during the long service. I felt her small hands on my ankle. Spontaneously, she began massaging my bare feet, continuing without stopping until I was called up to take my baptismal vows. Just two days earlier, on Maundy Thursday, the congregation had reenacted Jesus' commandment at the Last Supper by washing one another's feet. My daughter's touch seemed a beautiful parallel, a symbol of the ways we are called to support and love one another as servants and companions in everyday, sweet, and unexpected ways.

This book is also about those who have been companions to me on this journey, and in particular, how my Christianity has been shaped by my husband's devout Buddhist practice. The teachings and meditations to which I have been exposed through him played a critical role in my conversion, including in my coming to know Jesus. Yet, while I appreciate and can learn from his tradition, an important step for me has involved committing myself fully to a single path. It's been about giving up the pick-and-choose, buffet approach to spirituality to which I used to subscribe.

Mostly, this is the story of how a deep and astonishing relationship with a living God slowly emerged and how through it, I have been guided and transformed. I have been led to a new identity, to conversion and to confirmation within the Episcopal Church. I have been pushed to challenge a persistent, dismissive resistance to Jesus and instead to embrace a love of him through the internal experience of our relationship. It's the story of how I began—with faltering steps—to apply Christian principles to everyday life in the first year after my conversion, including during an unexpectedly painful period in my marriage.

This journey began with a simple word. A word I wrote in my journal one day. The word was "Hello." A simple message to God that I wrote on a blank page. And the powerful answer I received back was: "Hello."

PART 1

learning to listen

CHAPTER 1
the still, small voice

> "The Lord passed by, and a great and strong
> wind rent the mountains...but the Lord
> was not in the wind: and after the wind an
> earthquake; but the Lord was not in the
> earthquake: and after the earthquake a fire; but
> the Lord was not in the fire: and after the fire a
> still small voice."
>
> –1 Kings 19:11-12, KJV

MY DAUGHTER'S FACE was beet red. She had clawed her way into the bottom shelf of our linen closet where she was screaming, curled up in a fetal position. The latest epic tantrum of our resident three-year-old was waylaying the family plans. My stepson needed a ride to the movies, I had to submit a project for my online graduate course in a few hours, and my husband was trying to fix our washing machine that had frozen mid-cycle. It was pretty much a typical Saturday.

Three years before I was baptized, during the period when I heard God's voice distinctly for the first time, life was especially busy. In addition to being in graduate school part-time and juggling family life, I was working an intense, demanding job. Time was scarce, with school assignments and family chores filling up most weekends. Craving solitude and rejuvenation, I would turn to my journal, seeking a quiet hour here or there to try to become centered again. During one of these times, after dashing off a list of frustrations, hopes, and uncertainties, I found myself pausing and unexpectedly addressing an external presence in my journal—namely, God.

Up until that point, God had not been a regular part of my life. I had been raised in a Unitarian Universalist congregation outside of Boston. Although the community had many of the trappings of a mainstream church, there was actually no obligation in the diverse group to adhere to a particular religious doctrine or even to believe in God. The group welcomed Pagans, Spirit-seekers, and atheists alike. The central creed became a commitment to social justice, and the community rallied around numerous liberal causes. Members joked that for them, the Holy Trinity was "reduce, reuse, recycle." In this context, I wasn't given any roadmap of how to have a relationship with God. It was a dichotomy: Throughout my childhood and adolescence I was seen, known, and nurtured by this group, yet I wasn't offered any real religious compass. Racing with my brothers though a crowded sea of legs during coffee hour with adults smiling down at us, I felt a deep sense of belonging. In Sunday school, I learned songs with messages of peace, justice, and unity. As a teenager, the message I got from adult mentors was that my ideas mattered; my precocious search for meaning was embraced. The ethic in the congregation was to honor diversity and learn from the world's traditions. As such, most religions were treated with a respectful, if somewhat detached, carefulness.

Yet perhaps because so many members had fled to this group after being wounded by painful upbringings in the church, Christianity was treated differently. Unlike the other major religions, Christianity was often approached with a casual irreverence. When it came time to put on a Christmas pageant, the middle school students were allowed to write their own script. One year the title was, *Jesus: the Lost Years.* The resulting play was a kaleidoscope of characters that included the Grinch and Santa as a gay couple raising Jesus as a teenager in Los Angeles. The actor playing Jesus slumped around the stage wearing dark sunglasses and sagging pants, while Santa and the Grinch nagged and fussed over him. I imagined that the scene would have caused anyone's Christian grandmother visiting for the holidays to blanch.

I had remained an active member of the Unitarian Universalist church throughout my adolescence and into adulthood, joining the local congregation when I moved to Chapel Hill, North Carolina after college. Like most members, I was attracted to spirituality in general, loosely defined terms but remained skittish about anything that seemed dogmatic or supernatural. When someone lit a candle during the service for an ailing aunt or lost job, we were asked to keep the person "in our thoughts." Prayer was rarely mentioned. In this context, addressing God in my journal through writing was a new experience and not one for which I had any model.

Instead, the urge to address God in this way emerged spontaneously. I followed the impulse. That morning on a blank page in my notebook, I wrote, "Hello." I paused and there, to my surprise, was the response: *Hello.* It was an inner voice—not something external that I could hear audibly. Yet it was a distinct internal response from within me that somehow felt different from my regular mental chatter. I wrote the word down.

Then came another unexpected impulse. Without thinking, I wrote on the page, "I love you." And back came: *I know.* Again, I wrote the response down. I was taken off guard—this experience was completely unfamiliar. At the same time, I felt a spark of delight, a small flash of recognition and connection. In the weeks and months to come, this became a routine; I would write to God in my journal and would feel a response. A response inside me, yes, but at the same time, somehow distinct from me.

Over the next year, I began to sense the inner voice of this external presence more frequently. I found myself desiring more, wanting to cultivate this nascent relationship. I was uncertain if the Unitarian Universalist church could help me go further, so I signed up for a year-long group that was being offered for members who wanted to develop a regular spiritual practice. Some participants chose meditation; others took long walks in the woods or read poetry each morning. I made a commitment to praying daily. After reading about different approaches and styles of prayer, I adopted a multi-step practice which included time for thanksgiving, confession, intercession for others, petitions for my own needs, and then listening for God's response. Remarkably, in those quiet moments, I continued to feel God's presence.

Overall, things seemed to be going well. I had come to the class with a restless uncertainty of whether I should seek out a new spiritual community that would provide a more structured roadmap of how to get closer to God. But because of the positive experiences I'd been having with the group, I decided I would stick with my current congregation. I felt supported by the members of the class; my prayer practice was on track. I would stay put.

However, since God was increasingly becoming a compass in my life and this issue affected our relationship directly, I figured I ought to pray about it. When I did, I had a profound experience—so strong that it felt like a conversion moment. I felt God—through an inner voice in my mind—tell me to go in the opposite direction of what I had planned. When I told God my plans to stay put in my current community, the response I got back was: *No.*

The voice went on: *You can go deeper. Other places will have you go deeper.* More than surprised, I was exasperated.

This was not the plan...not *my* plan. I thought: Well, if I'm really listening to this inner voice, I am going to go for it and argue back. So my response was, "But this is my community. I want to get closer to you. Can I do that here?" The answer back: *No.*

I grabbed a piece of paper and started writing down this dialogue because it was so clear and compelling. *You need a place that will teach about me. The search isn't over.* And then, *You need confidence in me. What you need is teaching on how to be with me.* What was so striking was not just the stark clarity and strength of this message, but the fact that this internal voice contradicted my own agenda. It flew in the face of my own plans and opinions about how things ought to unfold.

To the non-believer or skeptic, I appreciate that this description might sound crazy or, at the very least, it would seem obvious that this so-called God voice I identified was actually just my own internal narrative. Clearly, I was feeling some ambivalence about my religious path, and, the skeptic would say, I was just dialoging with myself. All I can say is that the response I received felt distinct from me. I know what the chatter of my own brain sounds and feels like. This was different.

In the Old Testament, we read about how Elijah heard God speak with a "still, small voice" (I Kings 19: 12, KJV). For me, this voice is the quiet answer I sometimes hear in my own heart when I ask a question and can discern a response from a presence that is within me, yet bigger and different from me. In *When God Talks Back*, Luhrmann describes it as the "not-me" perception of prayer. She observed that for Christians who described a personal relationship with God, "if a thought felt spontaneous and unsought, it was more likely to be identified as God's. God's words 'popped' into the mind."

In trying to understand this as an anthropologist, Luhrmann compares the experience of discerning the difference between one's own thoughts and the inner voice of God as similar to learning how to recognize distinctions between various types of wine. She describes the "sudden recognition of the difference…between peppery versus smooth, cherry versus peach, flabby versus taut" flavors. As someone who only buys the cheapest wine, this sounds ridiculous to me. The possibility that there's a true difference between "masculine," "angular," and "flinty" wine seems improbable, even laughable. But I've never tried to discover or experience those distinctions. Through her research, Luhrmann found that some people—quite a large number of people, it turns out—report they are able to recognize the subtle distinction between their own thoughts and God's voice within their own minds.

In her popular book, *Eat, Pray, Love*, Elizabeth Gilbert describes a similar process of hearing God's voice. One night, in the depths of despair over her failing marriage, she asked God for help, and the response she got back was, "Go to bed." She had an immediate conviction that the message she received from the "omniscient interior voice" was real because the instructions weren't grand or sweeping but rather had the ring of simple authenticity.

I have to admit, when I read her description, I felt a bit indignant. My reaction reminded me of the experience people have as teenagers when they fall in love with a band before it becomes known and popular. And then when everyone else in the world starts to like the same band, they huff, "I loved that band before anyone else did!" I felt some of the same defensiveness: I had listened for the subtle but compelling voice of God within me before I knew anyone else was doing it. Before I knew it was a real *thing*.

Now I felt compelled to honor the mandate I had received in my prayers to find a religious community that could provide more guidance, structure, and role models. But where to go? It had been two years since I had first heard the quiet "hello" from God and written the word on a blank page in my journal. Now, it seemed that God had a new religious path in mind for me—but what? Was I to become a Christian? A Jew? A Sufi? At that point, while I felt a strong connection to God, I didn't know Jesus at all. I told a friend that I felt open to knowing Jesus, but he felt like a complete stranger to me.

CHAPTER 2
taking and giving

"Supposing God became a man—suppose
our human nature which can suffer and die
was amalgamated with God's nature in one
person—then that person could help us. He
could surrender His will, and suffer and die,
because He was man; and He could do it
perfectly because He was God. You and I can
go through this process only if God does
it in us; but God can do it only if
He becomes a man."

–C.S. Lewis, *Mere Christianity*

WHAT ARE THE WAYS God speaks to us? I had begun to
hear God through an internal voice, when I could still the
constant mental chatter and discern a distinct presence
in my mind. But frequently, even when I could quiet
my thoughts and tune into an awareness of God, I did
not sense a response when I posed a question or tried to

initiate a dialogue. Instead, my questions were met with silence. These moments weren't discouraging, however; in the months that followed, I began to experience other ways of "hearing" God. I started to feel guided here and there by a nudge, an impulse that somehow felt stronger than my own typical intuition.

I lay in bed one morning, several months after the dramatic prayer experience when I had heard an inner voice telling me to go in a new direction. Staring at the ceiling, I wondered what the next step would be. I felt like I was expecting my deployment papers, with no idea when or where I'd be assigned. For weeks, I had been trying not to be impatient, but that morning I was hoping for some answers. I sent out a silent request for help. Almost immediately, I had an overwhelming sense that I should call my father. I hesitated. I was unaccustomed to talking with my dad about spiritual matters. I squirmed beneath the comforter. What was I supposed to tell him? That a mysterious inner voice was calling me to embark on a new spiritual path? What was he going to say to that?

Yet, my father was probably in the best position to understand what it's like to embrace a dramatic personal transformation, to make a major pivot in the middle of one's life. My father has undergone two major conversions. First, he started off as a Communist and then ended up a Republican. Second, he became Catholic after thirty years as an agnostic Unitarian Universalist. It would be difficult to say which was more of a dramatic change.

My dad became politicized during the Vietnam War. His number came up early in the national lottery. From a privileged background, his father pulled strings to get him into the National Guard. He was sent to South Carolina for general basic training and spent sixteen weeks side-by-side with poor, uneducated guys who were going to be sent out to get killed. In contrast, my father would be returning to the ivy towers of law school. The profound unfairness changed him. When he returned to Harvard, he wrote for an underground newspaper, organized political protests, became a card-carrying communist, and fell in love with my mom. She was a quintessential hippie and activist, arrested soon after their first date for lying in front of supply trucks outside of a military center. They married, and after he graduated, my father started a law practice with two other like-minded attorneys. In addition to only charging clients what they could afford, my father and his colleagues paid themselves salaries on a sliding scale based on need. My mother was an elementary school teacher, and because my father was the only person in the firm who had another wage-earner in the family, he got paid the lowest annual salary—eight thousand dollars a year. The single guy who didn't have another income to rely on earned twelve thousand. The firm worked for the Teamsters union, and later my father served as an aide to one of the country's most left-leaning Congressmen. When my parents decided to start a family, the Unitarian Universalist church—which provided a liberal, non-dogmatic perspective on an individual's pursuit for truth and a strong focus on social justice—seemed a good place to raise their children and find a sense of community.

But while my mother remained a liberal activist, my dad's perspective transformed radically in the subsequent years. Wanting his kids to have the same opportunities he'd had, he took a job as an attorney for a computer corporation. Over the years, he became more fiscally conservative. Then his political views began to lean to the right. While my mother spent her time protesting unjust prison sentencing and fundraising for nuclear disarmament, my father switched jerseys and started voting with the other team. My mother's head was spinning. Was this the guy she'd married?

Yet somehow, miraculously, they stayed happily married. Mostly because they made an explicit agreement not to discuss politics over the dinner table—or really, at any other time, day or night.

Deeply intellectual, my father immersed himself in the writings of leading social conservatives of the day. Along the way, he was exposed to Catholic writers that inspired him. What began as a political journey ended with a powerful religious conversion. He never talks about the details. All he'll say is, "I had an encounter with Jesus that literally brought me to my knees." He was confirmed into the Catholic Church at the age of fifty-nine.

I adore my dad, but politically I'm unquestionably aligned with my mom. At the time of his conversion, I couldn't relate to his new religiosity. Christianity felt like a complete unknown, and since his politics and religion seemed to be all mixed together, I worried that our approach to spiritual exploration would be like oil and vinegar. Yet, that morning, there was a nudge.

So, I called him. I was traveling for work that day, and I reached him from a crowded airport in the evening. The words came out in a rush. I told him about hearing God calling me in a new direction, but I didn't know what that meant. I was open to Christianity, but I confessed I just didn't understand Jesus. I didn't *get* it. If I experienced a sense of God's presence in my life, why did I need an intermediary?

My dad didn't act like I was crazy. And he didn't launch into a lecture about who Jesus is and what he's all about. Instead, he advised me to read *Mere Christianity* by C.S. Lewis. He had given me a copy for Christmas five years before, and since then, it had sat on my bookshelf, untouched. My dad had never proselytized, never tried to convince me and my brothers to check out his religion, to give it a try. The only thing he ever did was to present each of his three children with a copy of this book, without any real explanation other than to say briefly that it had meant a lot to him. Now, that day on the call, he simply said, "Skip to the second part. It's what helped me get Jesus for the first time."

When I got home from my trip, I took the book down off the shelf. Lewis explains that the process of conversion and repentance is a return to God after acting as if we each belong only to ourselves. We have to give up the ironclad grip we maintain on our sense of self-determination, he says, and let God's will take center stage. The parts of ourselves that want to stay in control and be the star of the show have to die. But how does this happen? We're so imperfect that we don't have the tools to change our persistently self-obsessed ways on our own; we need God to do it in us and for us. However, there's a catch. Lewis writes, "We now need God's help in order to do something which God, in His own nature, never does at all—to surrender, to suffer, to submit, to die.... You and I can go through this process only if God does it in us; but God can do it only if He becomes a man."

Something clicked. For the first time, I had a mental map of why Christ is so necessary. Jesus is both the ambassador and the bridge, providing the pathway between our delusion and brokenness and God's perfection. Yet, while this intellectual understanding felt essential and even transformative, it still felt like only half of the equation. Having a mental construct is not the same as *experiencing* him, I thought to myself. It's not the same as how I felt God as a strong internal presence. Without that, I worried that any relationship with religion would feel like an empty shell.

✸ ✸ ✸

All this time that I was fluttering around, uncertain of where I was heading spiritually, my husband was on a strong and steady course. After traveling to Nepal as a young man, David became a serious scholar and practitioner of Mahayana Buddhism. While I was without a compass, he had been on a committed and structured path for almost twenty years. I observed his dedication and clarity with envy. For the first few years of our marriage, David shared Dharma teachings with me, quietly hoping I would convert. Yet, although I admired the Dharma philosophy, I somehow knew Buddhism was not my path. One of our daughter's children's books concludes with the lesson: "You just can't turn an apple tree into an orange tree." The insight resonated, although I still didn't have any certainty about what kind of tree I was meant to be.

Meanwhile, there were elements of Buddhism I deeply appreciated, and so I incorporated pieces of David's tradition into my life. Most significantly, I was drawn to a practice called "Taking and Giving," also known as Lojong in the Tibetan tradition. The goal of Mahayana Buddhism is to develop a mind of Bodhicitta, the desire and motivation to achieve spiritual liberation so that you can alleviate the suffering of others. To do this, we have to give up the normal self-preoccupation that drives us to spend our entire lives trying to manipulate external circumstances so that we'll be happy. Instead, we develop deep compassion. Through the practice of Taking and Giving, you imagine all of the pain, disappointment, and hurt that others experience becoming black smoke. You visualize breathing the smoke into your heart and bearing the burden yourself. This process destroys self-cherishing and allows you to breathe out happiness as a radiant light to others, one that doesn't just bring a temporary happiness to the recipients but permanently liberates them from suffering. This imaginative practice is just a dress rehearsal. The teaching tells us that we all have the capacity to become Buddhas who can do this very thing for real.

I feel the pain of the world keenly. I have a deep awareness that there is an "ocean of suffering," as the Buddhists say. And, much to my chagrin, it seems pretty hard to make much of a difference when faced with this ocean of overwhelming need. I started practicing Taking and Giving regularly for a couple of years with a sense that it provided a partial answer to the puzzle of how we get at the root of the problem of human suffering. Beyond just visualizing that I was breathing in the suffering of loved ones—close family and friends—I would widen my circle to imagine taking on the suffering of acquaintances, strangers, and those with whom I had conflict. Surprisingly, I found that this practice had the opposite effect of what one might imagine. Rather than feeling poisoned or burdened by this intense visualization, I would feel lighter and more peaceful after doing it.

One afternoon, David casually commented that the process was similar to what Jesus did. He took the suffering of all humanity into himself. And in doing so, he turned everything upside down. This comment reverberated in me. I tucked the insight away.

* * *

Still not knowing what God's plans were for me, I continued to play the waiting game. Then one day, that all changed. Jesus showed up in my consciousness, vividly and for the first time, when I was sitting on a cushion at my husband's Buddhist temple.

Earlier that weekend, I had begun to feel an unexpected and unnerving restlessness, a disquiet I couldn't quite explain. I asked David if we could go meditate at the center where he practiced. I was hoping that the quiet there would seep into my bones. After arriving, I settled down and began to imagine breathing in the suffering of both loved ones and of unknown strangers who I'd heard about on the news.

Suddenly, unexpectedly, Christ was present in me. I felt him and felt the Cross, as if they were superimposed on top of my body. His arms, torso, and legs were overlaid on mine. His presence was like one of those plastic sheets in an old overhead projector, generating a whole new image onto the scene. I was breathing in the suffering of others, but now he was inside of me, and I was doing it *through* him. He was not only helping me; I knew that fundamentally he was in charge. The black smoke entered my lungs, but it was as if it was filtered through him first. The peace that I was breathing out to others was not something I could generate within myself; it was a peace that only he could provide.

Most of all, it was like a light switch had been flipped. Jesus was no longer just an idea or a theoretical construct. He was suddenly in my consciousness. He was in my mind, yet as a distinctly external presence.

I stood up shakily. As tradition dictates, I automatically bowed to the photograph of the Buddhist teacher who is the head of the lineage of which David is a member. In the photograph, the teacher has piercing eyes that somehow both twinkle with merriment and hold you with unwavering expectation. To me, the image had always exuded a sense of tough love. That day, his gaze seemed to bore through me. And I suddenly had the sense—a deep knowing—that the Spirit had worked through this Buddhist teacher to touch my life. I felt clearly that I had been given the grace to know Christ through this non-traditional path. The eyes of the teacher in the photograph continued to sparkle. He approved.

It was the day before Easter. In the months to come, I was amazed to discover that once Jesus was in my consciousness, he never left. One year later to the day, I was baptized as a Christian in the Episcopal Church.

CHAPTER 3
tongues of fire

"When the day of Pentecost had come, they were all together in one place. And suddenly from heaven there came a sound like the rush of a violent wind, and it filled the entire house where they were sitting. Divided tongues, as of fire, appeared among them, and a tongue rested on each of them. All of them were filled with the Holy Spirit and began to speak in other languages, as the Spirit gave them ability."

–Acts 2:1-4

MEREDITH SHOWED UP on my doorstep wearing a bright red dress. It was a Sunday morning almost two months after Jesus had taken up residence in my consciousness. I hadn't met Meredith before, but she had recently married Ray, a family friend. Ray's daughters from his first marriage were close with my stepson, Soren, and they were picking him up for a beach trip for the kids' spring break. It was

Pentecost Sunday, the anniversary of the Holy Spirit descending fifty days after Easter. Meredith explained that she had just come from church and, following tradition, she was wearing the fiery color that represents the Holy Spirit.

As she stood in my kitchen, waiting for Soren to get his bags, Meredith didn't say much. I knew through the community grapevine that she had been widowed when her first husband had died after a long, painful, and expensive battle against cancer. She had fallen in love with Ray two years later, but we'd heard that the pain of her first husband's death was still fresh. Despite the losses she'd suffered, I was immediately struck by Meredith's presence—she had a peace and centeredness that were palpable. She seemed to exude a quiet joy standing there, leaning against my kitchen counter. "I want what she's got," I thought to myself. I felt an impulse to check out her church.

In an attempt to figure out the next step on my path, I had been attending a church a few miles from my house. It was a perfectly nice congregation with a beautiful sanctuary and friendly people. Yet for whatever reason, it had been a bland, somewhat disconnected experience for me. So a few weeks after I met Meredith, I visited her Episcopal Church. I had low expectations; I was committed to trying to find the right fit and figured it could take a while. They were offering an introductory class that morning after the service for people who were preparing for baptism or confirmation. I decided to stay to observe.

Fifteen minutes into the class, I recognized that it was exactly what I needed. I felt a sense of coming home. I signed up for the course and never left. Looking back, it seemed that Meredith—in her bright red dress—showed up like the bird on the branch in the Narnia story, silently inviting me to take the next step forward on the path that God was laying out.

In the subsequent months, the sense of coming home in the Episcopal Church deepened even though the liturgy was totally unfamiliar. The rhythm of worship, the centrality of scripture and communion, the prescribed routine of the weekly ritual—all of it felt foreign. I wasn't sure how to connect until my mother came for a visit that fall.

* * *

According to my mother's stories, there are some remarkable women in my family tree. My great-great grandmother and namesake, Kate Waller Barrett—whose legacy I would come to know more intimately in the months to come—was a social reformer in the late 1800's. Her daughter and my daughter's namesake, Lila, was in many ways her opposite: She led a quiet life, circumscribed by chronic illness that limited her mobility. Her daily activities were generally contained within a four-block boundary in downtown Alexandria, Virginia. Unlike her mother, who was a prominent player on the national and international scenes, Lila's range of influence wasn't grand or sweeping. Yet she touched innumerable lives with a remarkable grace and warmth which my mother describes as manifesting with almost a visible aura of holiness. Everyone adored her. "My boyfriends would come back to visit Lila, long after we'd broken up. We weren't in touch, but they'd come back to have tea with her."

I'd heard stories about these women my entire life. I had a fuzzy awareness that their deep religious devotion had played a central role in shaping their unique paths. But the details were lost on me. Because my brothers and I weren't raised as Christians, the specifics of our ancestors' heritage lacked immediate salience. It wasn't until my mother came to visit my new church and attended a service at my request that it all fell into place. "I battle internally with every line of scripture that's read and almost every assertion that's made," my mother explained, describing her agnostic resistance to church teachings. "But I always start crying during communion. I went to an Episcopal high school, of course, and we would celebrate the Eucharist every morning."

"You went to an Episcopal high school?" I asked, startled that I could have forgotten this detail of my mother's life.

She reminded me that all the women in our family who had populated the stories of my childhood were Episcopalians. My great-great grandmother had married an Episcopal priest who later became the dean of the cathedral in Atlanta. Their daughter, Lila, had never missed a service at her small neighborhood church. My parents had been married in an Episcopal Church to make Lila happy. My mother looked at me sideways, incredulous that I could have forgotten these details. I shrugged apologetically. Christianity hadn't been on my radar before, and I guessed I never paid attention.

More importantly, the sense of home I felt in the church now started to make sense. Suddenly, I could feel the encouraging hands of these ancestors on my back. They were there to help as I slowly began the journey of understanding what it means to be a Christian. I could lean on their legacy. These people, all long dead, were becoming both the breadcrumbs on the path forward and the tail wind at my back.

How does God speak to us? I was starting to recognize some of the ways: through the still, small internal voice of a divine presence, through the nudge that is somehow bigger than normal intuition. But now I began to see how God speaks to us through the people who touch our lives and guide us forward. God speaks not just within us, of course, but between us, becoming the invisible arrows that connect us, stretching forward and back between generations. The "communion of Saints" is the term used to describe the community of the faithful who live now and who have come before us. They become an invisible backbone that lifts, strengthens, and stabilizes us on our journeys.

After Jesus' resurrection and ascension, the Holy Spirit first descended with a rush of wind and then with tongues of fire. These tongues of fire came to rest on each of the disciples. Jerusalem at the time was filled with people of every ethnicity and nationality. The Holy Spirit filled the disciples and gave them the ability to speak and to be heard in the native languages of all those who surrounded them. Scripture tells us that the people were amazed, astonished, and perplexed to be able to suddenly understand what these strangers had to say about God and God's powers.

But it is one thing to be able to understand someone standing right in front of us. How do we hear the voices of those in the communion of Saints who have died years ago? To facilitate these connections, the Holy Spirit becomes like a bike-riding courier who dodges his way through urban traffic so that we can receive our ancestors' precious messages. In my case, my relatives had been strangers to me. Because I occupied an almost exclusively secular world, I practically spoke a different language from these women. But the Holy Spirit stretched across that divide, laying tongues of fire out like a bridge so that I could hear and understand their silent offer—an offer to be there to help hold and guide me as I continued to figure out what came next.

So whether it is the neighbor wearing a red dress who shows up at the door one morning or a silent offer from those who have gone before, an important part of listening for God's voice seems to be about paying attention to the messages that come through the unexpected invitations in our relationships. It's about noticing and recognizing the moments of providence that make us slap our foreheads: "Amazing that she just showed up at my door one day!"

"How could I forget who my ancestors were?" "How crazy that I feel at home here." "Why didn't I see it all before?"

In my case, the knowledge that I could lean on the legacy of my ancestors and countless others who have gone before was comforting as I became accustomed to the rhythm of Christian worship—and particularly, as I tried to get to know and understand Christ. Because even though I had experienced him in my prayers and could feel his presence, I realized in the weeks and months to come the extent to which I still held Jesus at arm's length.

CHAPTER 4
abiding love

"The question 'Who is Jesus Christ for us?'
cannot be answered merely by information. It
is, therefore, more than a question, more of a
quest. When we find the answer to a question
we get on with other things. But to have a
quest is to possess the very thing that allows our
lives to go on, that calls us to follow after it.
Jesus Christ is not a question to be answered:
rather he is a quest to be lived."

–Herbert O'Driscoll, *Emmanuel: Encountering Jesus as Lord*

THE REALIZATION THAT I WAS keeping Jesus at arm's length—despite all my reading and prayerful efforts—came to me the day before I was scheduled to be confirmed in the Episcopal Church. I had been baptized exactly one week before, surrounded by family and friends. It was the culmination of a year of preparation and months of trying to discern whether I was ready to commit. I had gone back and forth, flip flopping like a fish on a dock, not sure what it would take to know—*really* know—that I was ready.

The answer had come one evening after reading the Catechism in the *Book of Common Prayer*, which is written in question and answer format. As my eyes fell on the question, "What is Holy Baptism?" the corresponding answer on the page spoke with striking clarity: "Holy Baptism is the sacrament by which God adopts us as his children." For months I'd been asking the question in my prayers: "Am I ready?" but I hadn't felt any conclusive response. There had only been silence. I realized in that moment that I had been asking the wrong question. Rather than inquiring about *my* readiness, I paused, closed my eyes, and asked God if He was ready to adopt me as His child. The answer came back simply, *I am*. This felt like the guidance I had been waiting for, and so I proceeded. A few weeks later, I was baptized at the Vigil service the night before Easter.

Seven days had passed, and we were preparing for the Bishop's annual visit to the church. I was to be confirmed as an Episcopalian with about thirty other parishioners, including twenty teenagers. We had gathered for a rehearsal and then stayed for a noon-day Eucharist service. It was only the third time I'd taken communion, and as I knelt down in prayer after I'd received the bread and wine, Christ was abruptly front-and-center in my consciousness. I had grown accustomed to experiencing Christ as a loving and approving presence, but this time, I experienced something new. Jesus seemed stern, expectant, even impatient. Why? I was confused. There I was, newly baptized, about to be confirmed. What was the problem?

As I continued to sit there, unmoving, I had an overpowering feeling that Jesus was waiting—not quite disapprovingly, but rather with unyielding expectation— with a definite sense of tough love. Perplexed, I figured I ought to pray about it. In my prayers, I felt a clear answer: Jesus was ready. Ready for me to lay down my resistance, the internal barriers I was keeping up between us. He knew I was keeping him at arm's length. He was ready for that to stop. Okay, I smiled. I could try to do that.

* * *

In Marcus Borg's *Meeting Jesus for the First Time*, he encourages readers to think back to what stories we were told about Jesus in our childhoods. The message I received about Christ was clear and consistent: "We believe that Jesus was a great teacher," the adults in my life would explain. "We just don't believe he was the Son of God." Other messages were communicated, too: stories about oppressive experiences within the Church, anger at hateful acts committed by Christians in God's name, uneasiness about religion in general. But I realized that the most corrosive element of the narrative that I received in childhood was not the discomfort, mistrust, or even the resentment toward Christianity that was expressed. Rather, the most damaging aspect was the persistent and profound dismissal of Jesus. Yeah, he was a good guy—

not much more than that. In his book, *The New Religious Humanists*, Gregory Wolfe describes that the "liberal error" of treating Jesus as "merely human" means that he "becomes nothing more than a superior social worker or a popular guru." The disregard of the possibility that Jesus could be anything more made it a difficult and intimidating transition for me to even consider Christ as God, particularly with heavy words like "Lord" and "Savior" thrown into the mix.

But I was slowly growing more open to experiencing the divinity of Jesus. A few months before my baptism, the opening words of John's gospel were read in church as part of the lectionary cycle: "The true light, which enlightens everyone, was coming into the world" (John 1: 9). That morning as the passage was being read, a bright ray of sunlight slanted dramatically through the window and streaked across my face. I felt my heart opening with a true commitment to really get to know Jesus. I was ready to lay aside my preconceptions and open myself to knowing him fully, wherever that might lead.

However, a lifetime of dismissing Christ was not so easy to overcome. As I was preparing for life as a Christian, I felt like I was in the middle of a wild and wonderful love affair with God. But when I was honest with myself, I admitted that I often felt frustrated with trying to know Jesus as God; I was full of a tense, almost queasy resistance. Somewhat reassuring was the well-known Christian writer Kathleen Norris' acknowledgment that when she first began attending church services as an adult, she "experienced Jesus only as a stumbling block." I, too, felt a block, even though Jesus had shown up dramatically in my prayers unbidden one day and had never left—lingering in the back of my consciousness, always present I realized, whenever I turned my attention his way. Even so, resistance remained. As it turned out, I wasn't fooling Jesus. It was the day before my confirmation, and he was ready for a change.

One challenge for me during this time had been a lingering confusion about how salvation through Jesus actually *works*. As I had read more about this issue, I was dismayed to discover that there's not an entirely clear consensus among theologians on that front. Multiple answers have been given to the question of how Jesus saves us, ranging from the view of "penal substitution"—that Jesus received the punishment we deserve in place of us—to the view that Christ's resurrection was the ultimate victory over death. Each explanation is seen by the experts as having limitations. This was discouraging. If preeminent Christian scholars couldn't come to clear consensus about the mechanism of how Jesus saves us, how did I have any hope of understanding it? C.S. Lewis provides some reassurance about this conundrum. In *Mere Christianity* he writes, "A man can eat his dinner without understanding exactly how food nourishes him. A man can accept what Christ has done without knowing how it works: indeed, he certainly would not know how it works until he has accepted it."

Lewis' argument made sense on one level. But it still felt risky and difficult to accept something—especially something so important—without fully understanding it.

Luckily, in contemporary life, we have the luxury of modern communication tools to assist with spiritual crises. I texted my brother Andrew and told him I needed help with Jesus. Andrew was in the middle of his own evolving conversion journey, farther along the path than me in many ways. Several years before, he'd moved to New Orleans to study jazz and gospel music and had gotten the opportunity to play piano for the oldest African-American Baptist church in Louisiana. He wanted the experience to build his musical skills, but he needed to get baptized to keep the gig. He took the plunge, literally, without really understanding what he was getting himself into. "It goes to show that God reaches out to us in mysterious ways, even when we're inadequate and don't fully understand what God is asking of us," Andrew says. Now, several years later, this path has blossomed into an authentic calling and a deepening faith and love for Christ. He reports that spirituality is the most important thing in his life, and Christ is the driving force behind it all. During the rest of his time in New Orleans, he played piano for the church every Sunday, the only white guy in the congregation. When I went to visit, it was overwhelming to see how much the members of the church loved him. The preacher prayed out loud from the pulpit for him and me, a stranger, during the service.

That day, Andrew texted me back and told me to read John 15. He knew that I was a total beginner when it comes to the Bible. Over the past year, I'd become friends with cradle Christians whose entire childhoods were steeped in scriptural study. They knew biblical characters as well as they knew their own family members and could pepper conversations with lengthy, memorized quotations. I think I was assigned a section of the New Testament once for a college class, but I had skipped the reading assignment that week. That was it. I didn't get any other real exposure. My ignorance now made me cringe.

But it was all about baby steps. I sat down with the Bible I had—the cracked copy my husband had received when he was twelve years old in the Protestant church his parents rarely attended. I had a strong desire to read the passage my brother recommended. But recently, I'd been meeting with a "spiritual director"—a counselor of sorts who'd been recommended by my priest and had been providing me with one-on-one support on the journey. Through a process of discernment together, we'd been figuring out the best way for me to get familiar with the Bible, to start to understand what it holds and what it could hold for me. I'd committed myself to the practice of *lectio divina*, or sacred reading, a process of listening for the ways God speaks to us through scripture.

Continuing with my unorthodox ways, I had a somewhat unusual approach even to this practice. Others read the Bible in order from start to finish, or follow a prescribed study schedule. Instead, through trial and error, I had started to use what I called the "Ouija board" method of Bible reading. It worked best if I could quiet my mind and try to let the Spirit work through me by intuition to select a scriptural passage. I would meditate, attempting to listen for God, and then slowly run my fingers along the edge of the pages until I felt called to stop and read.

I worried that this was a nutball approach, so for awhile I tried reading the Bible the other way—in a prescribed order every evening, with serious and concentrated discipline. But I started getting nightly headaches, a problem I had never experienced before. I didn't put two-and-two together until I discussed it with my spiritual director. She reassured me the method I had been using to select a Bible passage had been a common practice throughout history. Some famous Christians had used this more intuitive approach: Saint Augustine had his big conversion moment when he flipped open the Bible at random and read the first words he saw. When I used the intuitive method, the process led to surprisingly powerful results. I'd been deeply moved by ways that the words of the Old and New Testaments—chosen seemingly by chance—spoke to me in profound ways. I was starting to experience what it means to "hear" God through scripture.

That day, with my eyes closed, I ran my fingers along the edge of the pages until I felt a nudge to stop. I opened to John 15, the exact passage my brother had recommended to help me in my search to better understand Jesus.

The coincidence felt dramatic. My eyes flitted to the previous page, and the words of John 14 spoke to me first: "Do not let your hearts be troubled. Believe in God, believe also in me. In my Father's house there are many dwelling places." At the time, I received this as an invitation to see and understand God through all the "dwelling places" in which God exists—including, and above all, in Christ. And then, the text of John 15, with clarity and grace, came into my heart: "I am the true vine, and my Father is the vine grower. He removes every branch in me that bears no fruit. Every branch that bears fruit he prunes to make it bear more fruit. You have already been cleansed by the word that I have spoken to you. Abide in me as I abide in you." (John 15: 1-4)

I dwelled in the words, rolled them over in my mind, savoring them. I felt Jesus in me and experienced a shift. A warm love for him grew and suffused me—a friendly, open love that had been elusive before. I had been trying to pursue Jesus by finding the theological explanation of how it all works. How the two plus two equals four in the Jesus equation. And I knew that would be an important part of the journey. Yet as the writer Herbert O'Driscoll reminds us, learning to love Jesus is more than a process of gathering information about him; it is an ongoing quest. If I had all the answers I was seeking, the search would be over. I could tell the story and move on. But O'Driscoll compares the process of coming to know Christ to two people getting married. You can't enter into a marriage by listing all of the things you *believe* about it: that marriage will provide companionship and financial stability, or even that it's a worthy pursuit because it's a sacrament of the Church. Rather, you have to experience the love of your partner first, trust the reality and vibrancy of your connection. And then, after standing at the altar and saying "I do," you must spend a lifetime living into that relationship to really understand what marriage means and can be. Similarly, I will spend a lifetime trying to fully recognize who Jesus is and who he can be in my life. I had to learn to trust Jesus and love him *first*, rather than only approaching him by field testing various theological beliefs.

Once, early in my journey, after revealing to a non-religious friend that my spiritual life was really thriving, she asked me—not meaning to be unkind, but authentically curious—did I *really* believe in God? The question brought me up short; it felt like she'd dashed cold water over my head. Suddenly I was questioning myself—did I really believe? That week in church, the minister explained in her sermon that the question of whether she *believed* in God wasn't particularly helpful or illuminating. Instead, she focused on the *experience* of God's presence, and that is how she came to know the reality of God. To the inner critic who worries that this approach is anti-intellectual, Kathleen Norris reassures us that it is "not mindless at all. It is head working inseparably from heart; whole body religion." The day before my confirmation, when I felt Jesus' stern expectation in my prayers, I realized all the ways I kept the door closed to experiencing Christ as God in my life. I had thought the first step was to shore up my intellectual beliefs about how redemption and salvation all came together. But I realized that there would be time for that. In the meantime and as an essential first step, I let my defenses down and opened my heart to loving him.

Can I say that I never looked back? That my resistance to Christ never returned? No, the truth is that I find myself slipping back into disconnection and skepticism. Without fully realizing I'm doing it, I extend my arms out again to keep Jesus at bay. This is the ongoing journey that O'Driscoll describes which doesn't end with a single answer, but keeps going on and on throughout a lifetime.

A few weeks after my confirmation, I parked the car after taking my daughter to school. Turning off the ignition, I sat on the side of the road for twenty minutes in prayer before heading to work. I was surprised to feel Jesus' presence wash through me there on that ordinary day. I had the image of him literally settling himself in my body, fluffing and adjusting his robes as he got comfortable. "Abide in me as I abide in you." What an outrageous blessing that Christ has bestowed upon me, that he chose to abide in me, despite all my resistance and barriers. Since then, when I find myself holding Jesus at arm's length, the difference is that I know better than to dismiss him. Instead, I see it as my own shortcoming, not an opening to reject him. And thankfully, I have the opportunity to challenge and transform my resistance, as I return—again and again—to the experience of our relationship.

PART 2

learning to discern

CHAPTER 5

a call

> "The question is not what we intended
> ourselves to be, but what He intended us to
> be when He made us…. We may be content
> to remain what we call 'ordinary people': but
> He is determined to carry out a quite different
> plan. To shrink back from that plan…is laziness
> and cowardice. To submit…is obedience."
> –C.S. Lewis, *Mere Christianity*

THE DAY WHEN I ASKED God in my prayers for permission to stay put on the path I was on—the day God said "no" and called me in a different direction and ultimately to Christ—I also asked whether I was on the right track professionally. God and I were on a roll that day, and I figured I ought to try and get as many answers as I could. At that point, I was working for an international public health organization, helping to increase access to birth control in developing countries. But knowing that my connection to God was growing stronger and that I was being called in a new direction, a secret thought emerged. A flirtation with a half-conceived question. "Do you want me to become a minister?" I asked. The answer was a quick and definitive, *No.* Okay, I decided to try another question. "Is your calling for me to work on reproductive health?" Immediately, the simple answer came: *Yes.*

I had experienced a similar affirmation of my current work the previous year. I was in the middle of a job search. I had interviewed at the public health organization and had a great connection with the hiring managers. It was one of those falling in love moments similar to what I'd experienced as an eighteen-year-old during my interview with an admissions officer at the college I ended up attending. This was it; I wanted this one. But they hadn't called me back to let me know if the job was mine or not. They told me to expect a call on Tuesday afternoon, but the call hadn't come. I was disheartened. I started to go to a dark place mentally. During an instant message chat with my brother, I tried to ward off the ego-crushing thoughts that were threatening to invade. I began to type over and over again in the chat window: "I want that call. I want that call." It became a mantra. I logged off the computer and climbed into the shower. As I stood with the water streaming over me, I began—without really intending to do so—to talk to God. The mantra continued, but now I was addressing God. "I want the call. I want the call. I want the call." And suddenly, I had the striking insight:

I didn't just want the call from Human Resources about this position. I wanted The Call. I wanted my calling.

With the legacy of the peace and justice movements of the 1960s shaping my cultural upbringing, there was always an expectation from my mother and within my community that I would focus my work on making the world a better place. In my twenties, I struggled with these messages. How the heck do you actually *make* the world a better place? The non-profit organizations that I worked for right out of college seemed dysfunctional, ineffective, and even self-serving. I didn't want to be part of that. I had a deep desire to help be a catalyst for meaningful, impactful social change, and I became more and more frustrated as an effective model for this change remained elusive. But I'd never conceived of my desire as the longing for a "calling." That wasn't my framework.

Yet, the mantra in my heart that day in the shower as I spontaneously prayed to God felt strong and true: I wanted my calling. I wanted a call that was bigger than me.

I got out of the shower. I wrapped the towel around my body, and before I could dry off, the phone rang. It was the HR representative. I got the job.

* * *

So a new chapter began in my life of working in an international arena to help increase access to birth control. The work was challenging and exhilarating. I recognized more and more the importance of women around the world being able to control their own fertility, including and especially women trapped in a cycle of poverty. There was the woman I met in Uganda who had six children by the time she was twenty-four. She loved her kids and wanted desperately to avoid another pregnancy so that she could take better care of the family she already had. I saw how access to birth control touches on every area of health and development: maternal and child health, environmental sustainability, gender equality, the economic advancement of families and communities.

At the same time, a painful drama was playing out in my own life. The sweet, funny, gentle man I had fallen in love with in my mid-twenties was sixteen years older than me. Although I had fretted about the age difference, David and I were a great fit—he was a true love and best friend. We married, and I became not just a wife but a stepmother to Soren, the son from his first marriage. About a year later, we had a baby girl. On an accelerated timeline because of the age difference, I hadn't been sure if I was ready to have a baby. Yet when my daughter Lila was born, I felt the rightness of it. I felt *good* at being a mother in a fundamental, beyond anxiety, soul-fit kind of way. I knew I was made to be a parent. Within weeks of Lila's birth, a restless desire blossomed in me for another baby. I wanted more of the amazing miracle of motherhood.

But David was in his late forties, and we had two kids. He had no interest in having another. He felt our lives were already stretched too thin. Over the next four years, we negotiated, listened, debated. I cried, was comforted, and then cried some more. Through it all, we were respectful and loving. We didn't suppress our own desires or blow off the other person's. We handled the dilemma with skill and patience. In some ways, this made it worse. There was no one to blame, no one to hammer with the full blast of my anger and disappointment. As the conversations continued, there was still no consensus. After careful discernment, David felt clear that he didn't want another baby. What was I to do? The internal pull for another child was relentless; it was a daily obsession, a clawing hunger.

At the same time that I was promoting birth control around the world, birth control was preventing me from having the very thing I wanted most. The irony was not lost on me.

An opponent of contraception who objects on religious grounds might conclude that I was flying in the face of God's will by altering my fertility with a modern contraceptive method. Indeed, in her book *Where There is Love, There is God*, Mother Teresa wrote, "In destroying the power of giving life through contraception one…is paying attention to self and so it destroys the gift of love in him or her."

However, rather than "paying attention to self"— honoring my own wants and needs—through the use of birth control, I was attempting to be loving and responsive to David's desires. In the months after my baptism, I realized that I also needed to make sure I was being responsive to God's will in this matter. What did God want?

On a family trip to Vermont early that summer, I decided that perhaps there was something symbolic I could do to let go of the struggle. I would ask God for help to release the obsessive longing into the waters of the lake by which we were vacationing. I paddled out into the middle of the water in a kayak. I scrunched my face and tried to conjure up my best visualization of what it would feel like to let this relentless desire for a baby simply float away.

To my surprise, the image of a grown man sprang into my consciousness—a man with curly brown hair and a laughing face. Suddenly, what spontaneously filled my imagination was a visualization of an adult with a fully formed, detailed narrative. Compelling details about this fictitious person came unbidden into my mind. He had a garden; he'd written two books; he had two daughters and a wife. Who was this person?

I suddenly knew that this was the adult version of the baby I could have. Saying no to getting pregnant meant saying no to this person—to this life story. How could I possibly do that? Was he waiting and wanting to be born?

In my imagination, I began to dialogue with this person. I asked him, "Do you want to be born?" He replied simply, "No, I'm okay to skip this life. I'm ready to be with God."

What? Startled, I asked again, "Do you want to be born?" The response was loving, playful. No, he really was okay skipping this life. What ensued was a long, internal conversation. A back-and-forth with this imaginary guy who had emerged out of nowhere. He fully knew the life he could have that he was giving up. He wanted to be with God. He reassured me. He joked with me. As the sun set over the Vermont lake, the water became streaked with reflected red and golden light. I had the sense that Christ was coming down to get this man who had appeared in my mind's eye. I also felt that Mary was there with Jesus, waiting. I'd never given much thought to Mary before, except cursory recognition during Christmas caroling at friends' holiday parties. But there she was. Waiting to help love, guide, and care for this unborn child. "Go," the voice of this man said. "Go take care of Lila and Soren. I will be fine."

In my conversations with David up until that point, I had been talking with him about sacrifice. That my marrying an older man, giving up my dreams of having another baby—these were all big sacrifices. Sacrifices he didn't have to make, I pointed out with resentment. That day by the lake, I had brought a copy of Thomas Merton's classic *New Seeds of Contemplation*. As I prayed and dialogued with the person in my imagination, I flipped open to the middle of the book. Merton's definition of sacrifice was at the top of the page: "A sacrifice is an action which is objectively sacred...and what is important is not so much the pain or difficulty attached to it as the *meaning*, the sacred significance which...*effects a divine and religious transformation* in the worshipper, thus consecrating and uniting him more closely to God."

In my conversations with David, I'd been talking about my sacrifice as the burn of not getting what I wanted. But instead, could I re-imagine this sacrifice as an act of spiritual transformation? One that was part of a larger journey of growing closer to God? I flipped to another page at random, and Merton's description of Mary leapt out at me. Mary's "chief glory is in her nothingness." He writes, "As one who acted simply in loving submission to His command, in the pure obedience of faith…it is the faith and fidelity of this humble handmaid…that enables her to be the perfect instrument of God, and nothing else but His instrument."

I rowed back to shore, subdued. That night at the cabin, our extended family lay out in the yard after dinner. Everyone was chatting and joking, reflecting on a day of hiking, swimming, and shopping. I was quiet—I hadn't mentioned my experience to anyone. The night was calm. Most of the sky was dark, but the last rays of light illuminated the upper sky on the distant horizon when lightning began to flash in the furthest clouds. There was no sound—no thunder, no rain. The lightning did not reach down to the earth. Instead, it remained only in the highest clouds, blazing gold and deep purple. My family exclaimed with surprise. My mother who had been coming to Vermont since her childhood had never seen anything like it. "What was it called?" she asked. No one was sure. In that moment, a quiet certainty filled me. I knew with an inner, unshakeable confidence that the light show was a heavenly celebration. The child that I wouldn't have—who would never even be conceived—had decided to be with God. And God was celebrating.

The conversation I had that day with the imaginary, curly haired man all happened within my mind. It was internal—there was no audible or visual experience. No hallucinations, no talking out loud to myself. Someone could easily describe my experience as being a simple visualization, an outcome of a creative imagination. And it was. But it also felt real. Luhrmann describes that one of the ways people experience God speaking to them is with "mental images he places in [the] mind." This claim is enough to make almost anyone cringe with skepticism. Is it possible that an entirely subjective, internal reverie could legitimately be of and from God? How could one ever put one's trust in such an experience? Barbara Brown Taylor, the popular writer and theologian, acknowledges that even among religious people, placing one's faith in an imaginative prayer process is a risky proposition. She writes, "to suggest that conversion is an imaginative act is to risk not being taken seriously, because imagination has a bad reputation among people of faith.... It is a synonym for fantasy." But she goes on to argue that, in fact, the way we move beyond the world that we can see and touch with our senses into a reality that is permeated by God's presence is through our imaginations. "Over and over again," she writes, "the human imagination turns out to be the place where vision is formed and reformed, where human beings encounter an inner reality with power to transform the other realities of their lives."

That day, the images in my mind felt like they came unbidden—with an energy and strength that were bigger than me. It felt as though I'd really spoken, through an internal dialogue, to the spirit of an unborn son. And it felt like he really was okay to give up an earthly life which included the possibility of gardens planted, novels written, a marriage, and two daughters. He wanted to go and be with God. I was happy for him. And finally—after years of tearful negotiation with David—I found a slice of the peace that I had been looking for. The journey was not over—more soul-searching, more doubt, more unresolved resentment would follow. But for the moment, I knew that this was right.

So, when Mother Teresa says that contraception equals "paying attention to self," I respectfully beg to differ. For me, through this long journey, I listened to my own desires. But I also listened to others: my husband, the spirit of the child who could have been, and to God as I attempted to discern God's will though my foggy, imperfect lens. Birth control, it turned out, played a central role in allowing me to listen for and honor what seemed to be God's calling for me on this issue. And I saw how God celebrated the coming home of my son—God's son—with that silent, dramatic electrical lightshow one Vermont summer evening.

CHAPTER 6
at the table

"In a large house there are utensils not only
of gold and silver but also of wood and clay,
some for special use, some for ordinary. All
who cleanse themselves...will become special
utensils, dedicated and useful to the owner of
the house, ready for every good work."
–Timothy 2:20-22

A PAINFUL IRONY is that once we've gotten the very thing we've hoped for, we often become desperately afraid we'll lose it. In my case, I recognized that having a day job that both paid the bills and felt like a Spirit-filled calling was a rare and precious thing. This, in turn, created a heightened sense of anxiety. It raised the stakes. On one hand, I felt that I was in the right place at the right time; I was where God wanted me to be. On the other hand, I couldn't relax because now I wasn't just working some odd job. I was working My Job. So, what if I lost it? Our grant was scheduled to end in eighteen months. Then what? I had moved to North Carolina after college, and this is where David and I were settled. We were deeply rooted in the community, and Soren's mom, with whom we shared custody, lived nearby. I wasn't going to pick up and move to a global hub like Washington D.C. or New York City where jobs in my field were more plentiful. What if my employers kicked me out in the street? Would I be letting God down?

I had the sense to laugh at myself at this thinking. No pressure, right? I realized that these worries weren't helpful or even spiritually logical, but they lurked in the back of my mind on a daily basis.

My anxiety manifested in simple, everyday ways. I found that I was overly reliant on the whims of my boss, rather than trusting my path. Was I in her good graces that day? Did she assign me some task or did it go to another team member? I was wound up, and I perceived that it was affecting not just my sense of peace but my relationships with her and my coworkers.

A friend pointed out the fallacy in my thinking. "You're looking to your boss for an invitation to be at the table, to be a player," she reflected. "You don't need her permission. You're already at the table. Your life is the table. You can put your trust in that." Her advice resonated. I would try that view on for size.

★ ★ ★

In his book *Let Your Life Speak,* Parker Palmer describes how we must understand the ecology of our lives. Americans are taught that we can do anything, be anyone we want to be. That there are no limits. But in fact, God creates us as part of an ecosystem in which limits dictate our lives. Birds cannot swim, fish cannot fly, and neither can we be everything or do anything that we desire. That's not God's vision for us. In the ecology of our lives, Parker writes, "there are some roles and relationships in which we thrive and others in which we wither and die."

In his professional development workshops with teachers, Palmer asks participants to reflect on a time in the past few months when things were going well, when they felt in sync with their job and their calling. He also asks them to describe a time when they faced disaster—when they just wanted to quit and run far away from their life's work. As I went through this exercise on my own, I remembered a meeting I had attended just six weeks previously, during which I had felt deeply insecure. I had recently been assigned to work on a new project with a team of clinical scientists. While I sat as an observer through an important meeting, unfamiliar concepts swirled in the conversation around me. As a former Sociology major, the jumble of technical terms that the participants spouted off effortlessly were—as they say—Greek to me. I was in unfamiliar territory, and I was deeply unsettled to find that I couldn't contribute to the discussion because I couldn't even understand it. I was at the table, but did I belong there?

In the weeks after the meeting, a funk of insecurity settled around my shoulders. Every day—sometimes every hour—I questioned my position and value on the team. My skills were "soft." I could write, I could coordinate people and events, and I could think critically and strategically. But these skills seemed insubstantial compared to the scientists' skills. How did I articulate my role and its value to others—and also to myself?

In completing Palmer's mental exercise of reflecting on the dichotomous experiences in one's working life, I then thought of a moment when I felt fully engaged with my job. I reflected that in the weeks since the meeting during which I had felt so lost, I had played a central role in helping to galvanize the group to move their conversations forward into action. I was able to distill the scientific jargon and synthesize the group's thinking into a succinct summary document. I wrote text for a website and press release and made arrangements to have both posted online. We circulated an announcement about the project to over ten thousand people via listserves. As I reflected on this, I had a new appreciation for the ecology of my life. Yes, limits dictated my life. I wasn't and would never be a scientist. In my research organization, the scientists were at the top of the food chain. I was the product of a competitive culture; I thought my value would come from being at the top. But I began to see that God had a different vision for me. In reflecting on the ecology of our lives, Palmer writes, "God asks us only to honor our created nature, which means our limits as well as potentials.... One dwells with God by being faithful to one's nature. One crosses God by trying to be something one is not."

I continued to play with the image of being at the table as I tried to have faith in my sense of vocational calling. In my prayers one day, I quieted my mind and asked God for help. I opened to a page in the New Testament, and the section from Paul's letter to Timothy spoke straight to my heart: "In a large house there are utensils not only of gold and silver but also of wood and clay, some for special use, some for ordinary. All who cleanse themselves...will become special utensils, dedicated and useful to the owner of the house, ready for every good work" (Timothy 2:20-22).

I suddenly saw myself as one of these utensils the passage described—a spoon, made of wood or clay. A vessel lying on the table, ready for use. A spoon is not used for every meal, not needed for every bite. It is certainly not glorified, just an everyday domestic tool. But nonetheless it is essential to the meal, and not something that can be easily replaced or discarded. Similarly, I could see that all of the members of my team at work—and truly, each of us—are essential elements, with a place and a function at the table.

During this time, I was preparing for baptism. The priest explained that through the sacraments of baptism and communion I would be welcomed—permanently and with Christ's complete embrace—to the Lord's Table. Suddenly, the image of being at the table of *my* life shifted.

Yes, I was at the table. But truly and fundamentally, I was at *God's* table. Instead of worrying that my grant would end or that my job wasn't secure or anxiously seeking affirmation that my role was valued on the team, I could lie in peaceful repose, like a spoon on the table. Open and waiting for God's special use for me.

CHAPTER 7
vocations

"Our vocation is…to work together with
God in the creation of our own life, our own
identity, our own destiny…. To work out our
identity in God."

–Thomas Merton, *New Seeds of Contemplation*

As a new Christian, viewing God as the Creator-of-All-
Things did not come naturally to me. I could accept the
image of God as an omniscient and loving presence who
expressed opinions from the sidelines with the occasional
whisper or nudge on the shoulder. But a God who both
formed and animates the entire world? Despite my new
faith, I felt uneasy embracing this belief. Yet as I became
accustomed to my new life as a Christian, I decided
I ought to try to understand God as Creator, since this
is such a fundamental part of the Christian package. I
consciously decided not to spend time evaluating the

logic or probability of this view, but rather to act "as if." In Twelve Step programs, members are advised to act "as if" there is a Higher Power, despite any fundamental skepticism. Barbara Brown Taylor writes about this approach, arguing that "belief is less like certainty than like trust or hope. We are betting our lives on something we can not prove.... Most of the time the best we can hope to do is to live 'as if' it were all true and when we do, it all becomes truer somehow."

I found this approach appealing, and in applying it, I experienced remarkable effects. I began to have brief glimpses of what a new worldview with God at the center, as Creator, would look and feel like. Instead of driving home from work with a mind churning with unresolved dramas of the day, I found myself lifting my eyes up more often—noticing the world around me, viewing the lush trees lining the streets with deep appreciation for what I could view as God's creation as I tried to hold an "as if" attitude.

Walking in my neighborhood one evening, I came across a bed of irises. I bent to look at their frothy petals curling up and over one another in multi-layers of color and pattern. They were outrageous. Outrageous in their abundant beauty. Outrageously decadent. If God had created these irises—and I could feel in that moment that God did—God is truly outrageous in God's generosity and delight for this world.

Meanwhile, as I continued to struggle to understand the nature of vocation and calling, I kept praying for guidance. One day, I impulsively asked in my prayers if I should write a book about my spiritual experiences. This was a crazy question; I never had any ambition of writing a book before. But the answer that came bubbling back immediately inside of me was an unequivocal, *Yes.* Yet despite everything that had happened, it still felt strange to put my trust in this enigmatic interior voice. It was as though my mind were a dense forest, with each thought a tree crowded against its neighbor. This interior voice was like a face, barely visible in the far distance, popping out for a moment between the thicket of branches. It would have been easy to miss it—to just blink, shake my head, and glance away.

Instead, I began writing, carving out an hour here and there in the middle of a busy life. I was writing with an awareness that this was an irrational proposition. It was impractical to take on such a huge project without a clear vision of how it might fit into the bigger picture of my life or career. Still, in writing I felt a remarkable healing taking place. The persistent anxiety I felt about my job began to fall away. It was deeply reassuring to perceive another "nudge" from God about a possible next step on the path. It gave me hope that when my grant ended or if there were layoffs at work, I could trust that God would be there with another assignment, in whatever unexpected form it might take.

During that time, a friend from church, a dedicated and seasoned Christian, left a job in which she had been in a high profile, high status, twelve-month interim position.

I kept asking her sideways questions about whether she was sad to leave the job, secretly fishing for some sign of hidden resentment, grief, or fear. I wanted a voyeuristic glimpse into how she was handling the transition. But she just shrugged and smiled beneficently. "There's always God's next call." What wisdom and trust her simple response contained—a faith that in the midst of change and uncertainty, there would always be another calling. It might take a while for the nature and scope of the next assignment to become clear. God might pause for a long beat because there are things that can't be understood unless we experience the in-between places. But when the call comes, when it's time, our job is simply to respond with an open, willing heart.

In my case, I felt an unexpected sense of vocation in the writing. Samuel Wells, a well-known writer and priest in the Church of England, describes vocation as "a particular calling from God through which believers find their own place in the story of the redemption of all things." Wells explains that vocation is "not necessarily tied, or even closely related, to the duties of a job or the pursuit of a career. Nor is it necessarily static and permanent; it may develop and evolve over time. But it is tailored to a person's unique character and circumstances, and it invariably involves integrating the disparate and often confusing elements of someone's past experiences into a role that only they can perform, a gift that only they can give, a contribution that only they can make."

For me, it certainly did seem a bit audacious to suddenly take up a new identity as a writer, to take this call seriously, rather than just shrugging it off. It would have been remarkably easy—the path of least resistance, in fact—to fail to create the space in my life and in my busy schedule to explore where this "nudge" from the Spirit would lead. But isn't that always the temptation? To allow busyness or the sheer improbability of God's love to serve as the excuse that justifies allowing the call to slip right past us, unheeded?

When we consider the ecology of our lives, Parker Palmer advises us that we must not only acknowledge and embrace our limits. In addition, we must also embrace our potential and the possibilities that lie before us. He says we must "take the yes of the way that opens and respond with the yes of our lives." In learning to recognize God as Creator, I began to recognize how amazing God's gifts are, including the gift of a growing sense of vocation. Like the splashy white and purple layer cake of iris petals, the opportunity to tell my story is an outrageous gift from God. To this gift, I must say yes with the yes of my life.

CHAPTER 8

contradictions

"The most direct evidence for God—the
evidence of one's senses—is also the clearest
evidence for folly or madness."
–T.M. Luhrmann, *When God Talks Back*

SHORTLY AFTER A WHIRLWIND honeymoon to the
World's Fair in Philadelphia in 1876, my great-great-
grandparents moved to "Butchertown," a notorious
slum in Richmond, Virginia. Kate Waller, a vivacious,
restless nineteen-year-old, had fallen in love with Robert
South Barrett, the handsome, studious Episcopal priest
known for his passionate convictions. Having left the
comfort, familiarity, and affluence of Stafford County,
Virginia, where they had met, they were now living in
a neighborhood crowded with dilapidated houses and
tobacco factories in the small rectory beside the church.
One rainy night in 1878, soon after the birth of their

first son, a woman came to their door, begging for help. Standing in the doorway, soaking wet, the woman blurted out her story. She was also a new mother, but unmarried, a "fallen woman" who had been jilted by her lover when she had become pregnant. From a good family in a nearby town, the woman at the door had graduated at the top of her class. But now she was a social outcast, homeless and penniless, a disgrace to her family with nowhere to go. Kate invited the woman and her child into the house and gave them both a change of clothes. She laid the woman's baby on the bed to sleep beside her own son.

This encounter was a turning point in Kate Waller Barrett's life. More than two decades later, she wrote, "There the two babies laid side by side, my boy and hers… both innocent and pure; both equal in the sight of God; and yet in the eyes of the world, how different…. My boy, with every door open to him, with every hand stretched out to aid him; her boy, with every door closed to him…. And when I realized in this unequal struggle against this helpless, trusting, heart-broken woman…[that] good men and bad men, good women and bad women stood shoulder to shoulder to keep her down and out, and to make it almost impossible for her to be an honest woman and true mother—that the unjust laws of society denied to her the right to redeem the mistakes of the past by an unblemished future—my very blood boiled within me…. I heard, with startling distinctness, our Saviour's question to Simon, 'Seest though this woman?' Almost unknown to myself there entered into my heart at that moment a covenant with God that so long as I lived my voice would always be lifted in behalf of this outcast class, and my hand always held out to aid them."

I uncovered this writing when I was on a spiritual pilgrimage, retracing my ancestors' religious roots during the process of preparing for baptism. Throughout my entire life, I had heard the story about Kate Waller Barrett's encounter with the unwed mother. It was a pivotal moment; she heard and heeded the call she received. She went on to found a home in Atlanta for unwed mothers, which later became part of the national network of Florence Crittenton Homes, named after the daughter of the well-known philanthropist, Charles Nelson Crittenton. With an awareness that she needed additional training to better serve her cause, Kate Waller Barrett earned a medical degree in 1892, one of the first women in the country to do so. She later became the general superintendant and then president of the National Florence Crittenton Mission. She held numerous prestigious positions throughout her life, including Special Representative of the U.S. Bureau of Immigration in Europe, advising on women's issues; president of the National Council of Women; and delegate to the 1924 Democratic National Convention. In all of these roles, Kate Waller Barrett dedicated her life to improving conditions for her "fallen sisters."

In uncovering my great-great-grandmother's writing about her journey, two things jumped out at me. The first was her description of hearing "with startling distinctness" the words of the gospel as she witnessed the bitter suffering of the stranger in her home. This inner voice led her to make an unshakeable covenant with God, a covenant that informed her life's work. This vision of making a commitment to work for social justice in response to a deep and abiding call from the Spirit offered a striking new model for me. Having been raised with a mandate to "make the world a better place" but without any spiritual map of how to do so, I was starting to understand how one's work can be grounded in faith after carefully listening for and honoring God's call.

My great-great-grandmother's writing also revealed her early struggles in Atlanta to establish a home for unmarried mothers in the face of fierce opposition from the community. The city council passed an ordinance banning such a home, newspapers wrote articles against it, and even some members of a multi-denominational ministers' group were in opposition. People of *faith* worked zealously to obstruct her and her call. I had never heard that part of the story.

The temptation then, and now, is to dismiss offhandedly those who oppose us and our deepest convictions. At minimum, we see them as misguided. If they use their faith to form arguments against us or tell us that they are responding to their own call from God, we typically go a step farther, writing them off as crazies, kooks, or meanies. But is this attitude tenable? Suppose, hypothetically, that ninety-five percent of the people who opposed my great-great-grandmother's work *were* both meanies and hypocrites—ill-spirited people who didn't bother to listen for God's voice or even, in any meaningful way, to heed Christ's teachings. But, hypothetically, what if the other five percent of those who opposed her were people of conscience and spiritual discipline, who were moved by the Spirit? What if they sat down, got quiet, prayed—and felt within themselves a quiet, inner voice calling them to oppose the very thing that had become my great-great-grandmother's covenant? Is it plausible that theirs, too, could be an authentic call from God?

In the months after my baptism, as I continued to try to understand the nature of vocation, I couldn't help but wonder if the process of discernment was all just a fantasy. Maybe my perception that God had a specific plan in mind for me was just wishful thinking. If I were to trust that my work to promote birth control was an authentic, Spirit-filled calling, was I to conclude that somebody else who claimed to have received an opposing call must be deluded? This seemed like dangerous and hubristic grounds.

In recent years, contraception has reemerged as a contentious political issue in the U.S. People of faith fight tirelessly as advocates on both side of the issue. Perhaps I am naive, but I imagine that opponents of birth control (at least some of them) have done a lot of soul-searching in the process of discerning God's will for them on this issue. In 2014, one of the plaintiffs in a case seeking an exemption to the Affordable Care Act's mandate regarding contraception was Little Sisters of the Poor, an order of nuns who run ecumenical nursing homes for the indigent elderly. As much as I am a passionate champion of universal access to safe and affordable contraception, I don't think I can assume that my position on this issue reflects an authentic call from God while these nuns' position does not.

Why, then, would God give us all such widely diverse, even contradictory, callings? Are we to conclude that these contradictions prove that it's all just a fantasy? That we can't put any trust in the messy, subjective process of discernment?

Clearly, the practice of listening for and interpreting God's very subtle calling in our own hearts leaves us wide open to the risk of misinterpretation, or in the worst case, flat out delusion and abuse. This is a scary proposition. Scary for me, as I attempt to discern my calling responsibly. And scary that I have to be open to the possibility that another person's position opposing mine might actually be an authentic call, too, not something that I can dismiss out of hand.

The Episcopal tradition provides a framework for responding to this dilemma. According to John H. Westerhoff, Episcopalians uphold the "conviction that truth is known and guarded by maintaining the tension between counter-opposite statements." Over and over, Christianity embraces seeming paradoxes, including of course, the claim that Jesus was both man and God, and that God is both One and Trinity. All Christians must live with the paradox that we are commanded to strive for both holiness in pure and disciplined actions while simultaneously embracing an expansive hospitality that requires us to embrace those with different views and even disappointing actions. Episcopalians in particular, Westerhoff reminds us, have a long history of being "able to tolerate theological and ethical messiness." The Anglican tradition emphasizes the principle of *via media*, or the middle way. As part of this, Episcopalians rely on the "three-legged stool" of Scripture, tradition, and reason when making decisions and intentionally accept theological ambiguity.

I was coming to see that perhaps God gives us contradictory callings to provide us with the chance to grow into God's vision of paradoxical hospitality, creating the perfect playground where we, like children, must learn to get along. Learning to love not just our friends, but also our would-be enemies takes a lifetime of practice. Kathleen Norris writes that in churches and other committed spiritual communities, a polarized us-versus-them attitude is "risky business" because "the person you're quick to label and dismiss as a racist, a homophobe, a queer, an anti-Semite, a misogynist, a bigoted conservative or a bleeding-heart liberal is also the person you're committed to live, work, pray, and dine with for the rest of your life." Instead, we have to learn to use "the tools [which] Jesus Christ has given...to overcome the temptation to condemn one another." In this age of divisiveness, the true task, as we seek solutions to our disagreements, is to learn to accept contradiction within community and even within ourselves, and to embrace those contradictions with a full, forgiving, and abundant love. In this way, perhaps it makes sense that God would give you, me, and the guy down the street different callings. I have a feeling that God is less concerned about the nature of our disagreements on the playground of life than in how we respond to our conflicts and differences. Perhaps God is providing us with the opportunity to gain the spiritual skills to be loving so that through the process, we are transformed.

But we are left with a problem: While many of us try to engage in this slow process of inner transformation, we still have urgent social problems to solve. I and many others believe that women around the world desperately need access to birth control. Women around the world die every day in childbirth, often because births are spaced too closely together or because pregnancies have occurred too frequently. Do those of us on this side of the issue have the time or patience to practice compassion for those who oppose our efforts? This is the conundrum. The problems we face are urgent and plentiful, and it is tempting to try to steamroll our opposition in a rush to find solutions.

But again, another paradox emerges: On one hand, we should not wait until the controversies blow over; in the letter of James, people of faith are commanded to be "doers of the word, and not merely hearers who deceive themselves" (James 1:22). This means that we must act on faith—including enacting our calling after responsibly discerning it. Yet we must also always remember our most fundamental commandment to love our neighbors as ourselves. This means loving not just the unwed mother that my great-great-grandmother vowed to help, or the women in Africa I attempt to serve today, but also those who oppose us—those who are doers of a drastically different calling. And indeed, that is paradoxical, radical love at its very best.

PART 3
learning to follow

CHAPTER 9
putting God first

"My dear Wormwood, I note with grave
displeasure that your patient has become a
Christian…. There is no need to despair;
hundreds of these adult converts have been
reclaimed after a brief sojourn in the Enemy's
camp and are now with us. All the *habits* of the
patient, both mental and bodily,
are still in our favor."

–C.S. Lewis, *The Screwtape Letters*

ON THE EASTER MORNING the day after I was baptized, I felt
like a shiny, exuberant, newlywed bride. At church I sat
next to a parishioner who I knew vaguely but who hadn't
been at the service the previous night. She kept glancing
at me sideways, trying to figure out—I was sure—why I
had a huge, stupid grin on my face throughout the liturgy.
During coffee hour, she hurried over to me. "I just realized

that you were baptized last night! Congratulations. I wondered why you were glowing as bright as a Christmas tree!" The glow lasted all day as my family and I enjoyed a non-traditional Easter dinner of spaghetti and meatballs on the back porch, while my daughter and her cousins hunted for chocolate eggs in the fading, golden sunlight.

Then, like a cruel trick, it turned out that the baptism weekend didn't include a honeymoon—a chance to savor and absorb my deep sense of spiritual delight. That night, a work emergency came up. I plunged into a frantic exchange of emails and scrambled to arrange childcare for the next morning, after originally planning on taking the day off. Two days later, we were shocked to learn that my best friend and her husband, whom I both adored, were unexpectedly getting a divorce. Later that week, my last surviving grandparent slipped into a coma after a long illness and died a few days afterward. Not only was I grieving my grandmother's death and my best friend's divorce, I felt, quite selfishly, ripped off. The tidal wave of joy I felt over Easter weekend had evaporated into stress and sadness. I wanted that honeymoon!

I relayed all of this to a friend the next weekend over dinner. He smiled knowingly. "Yes, when you're on Cloud Nine with the Spirit, Satan comes crashing in to disrupt things. He's the foil."

Satan? As part of my baptismal commitment, I had promised to "renounce Satan and all the spiritual forces of wickedness that rebel against God." But I hadn't spent much serious time thinking about the devil or what this promise had meant. Yet, with the baptismal waters barely dry, it felt compelling to reframe the week's difficult events as a test, a challenge from a mysterious outside force that I had the opportunity to try to overcome, rather than just as a series of random, difficult events.

At the same time, I felt wary of interpreting roadblocks through a lens of darkness. I wanted to see the glass as half full rather than focusing on potentially imaginary adversaries. It seemed safer to keep my eyes fixed on God instead of on the possible ways "the enemy" might be working against me.

In the coming weeks, however, keeping my eyes fixed on God proved difficult. I was unnerved to discover I wasn't able to regain my equilibrium and instead was in an increasingly bleak and murky place. Work had accelerated to a breakneck speed. Each day felt like I was riding a toboggan down a steep and icy slope, without any space between meetings, emails, and deadlines to catch my breath or even look for an opportunity to slow down the pace. Meanwhile, as I explored the meaning of vocation, I was attempting to scratch out some time for writing, which felt like the next right step on my spiritual path. David had been incredibly supportive of my conversion journey every step of the way, but after my baptism, we got into a series of confusing, circular arguments about scheduling that left us both feeling raw and depleted. My preparations for baptism had taken a lot of my time and energy, and David had been looking forward to things quieting down. Yet now I was preoccupied with another time-consuming project. Finally, after another draining go-round, he vulnerably admitted he was somewhat jealous: jealous of the time I was devoting to my spiritual practice and my writing, of the earnest passion I was feeling for both. His tender admission was sweet on one hand, and it helped us grow closer as I responded with reassurance. Yet, it felt confusing as well. I turned my attention—partly out of guilt—to tending to our marriage. Time was tight; I couldn't do it all. Without consciously deciding to do so, I put my writing on hold. My prayer life, which had been an almost daily practice for several years, started to suffer.

The devils in C.S. Lewis' classic book, *The Screwtape Letters*, exchange a series of letters to one another outlining strategies to achieve their goal of "undermining faith and preventing the formation of virtues" among humans. These strategies primarily consist of embedding corrosive, misguided thoughts in people's minds about God and themselves. Their "reward" is "the anguish and bewilderment of the human soul."

Feeling my own bewilderment about an overly-busy life, I sat down one day and wrote God a letter. I described the pattern in our relationship that had emerged in the past few weeks. "I have to take care of my obligations to work first; I have to take care of my family first. Any little bit that's leftover, I will give to you, God." The upshot of this approach, I realized, was that the amount of time and energy leftover for God kept shrinking and shrinking, until it was almost non-existent. At nine o'clock at night, there were always other priorities: an unfinished grant proposal to work on, an inbox filled with emails to process, an unsorted pile of laundry to put away.

In one of his letters to Wormwood, Screwtape reassures him that "all the *habits*" of newly converted Christians "both mental and bodily, are still in our favor." It is appropriate that the word *habit* is emphasized. I recognized that as a new disciple of Christ, I must learn entirely new habits, which is understandably difficult since my old ways are entrenched and automatic. I tighten my body without thinking or even realizing I'm doing it—gripping the steering wheel as I rush through my commute or as I pound the computer keyboard—unconsciously slipping back into the belief that I am entirely in control or that the completed project or the esteem of colleagues is where I will find happiness and satisfaction.

By admitting that I'd been leaving only the leftovers for my relationship with God, I also realized with sudden clarity that there was another choice. The alternative commitment that I could adopt went something like this: "I absolutely cherish my husband and our family. I also love my work. I will continue to honor both, not turning my back on either. But I must put God first. First and foremost, I must devote myself to my relationship with God."

In articulating this new thought—this alternative possibility—my heart lightened, my muscles loosened. The murky heaviness that had been clouding my spirit for weeks suddenly cleared. Surprisingly, I felt about a hundred pounds lighter.

The subsequent weeks felt completely different. While I remained busy, I found small yet meaningful ways to "put God first," including through everyday interactions with family and coworkers. I also spent time reflecting on this dramatic shift, feeling surprised that a simple change in intention could make such a difference. Was is possible that the devil had taken advantage of my weakness, my naiveté and my fatigue to feed me the undermining thought that I could give God only the little bit of myself that was leftover? That this would be an acceptable strategy in a overly-busy life?

The Episcopal priest and writer Margaret Guenther has a similar take to Lewis on how the devil works to undermine us in completely ordinary ways. She imagines Satan saying: "I don't need magic tricks or scary outfits. I can just stay beside you and keep saying, 'No.' I can try to quench the God-spark within you or I can keep wheedling until you try to quench it yourself. You'll end up doing all the work while I just watch and keep you company."

Her words resonated. The "God-spark" was a perfect description of what I felt deep inside me, the light that had led me down this path in the first place. It also felt like the thing that had been so threatened in the weeks after my baptism—flickering with an unexpected vulnerability. The transformative effect of turning to prayer and calling to God for help was striking. The God flame in me seemed to burn with renewed strength as the devilish fallacy was replaced by a new, liberating intention.

After the Last Supper, Jesus predicts Peter's denial but then reassures him of the enduring help he will provide: "Satan has demanded to sift all of you like wheat, but I have prayed for you that your own faith may not fail; and you, when once you have turned back, strengthen your brothers" (Luke 22:31). It is not a coincidence that during the baptismal covenant, the congregation responds collectively to the question, "Will you persevere in resisting evil?" with the reply, "I will, *with God's help*." We can't do it alone. It is God's grace that gives us the strength to maintain our faith through and beyond the times of trial, and then in turn, to help provide strength to our brothers and sisters. It felt as though Satan had tried to sift me like wheat through his sieve in the months after the stunning spiritual high of my baptism, and I anticipated that I would be rolled around in that sifter at other times in the years to come. In the meantime, I was sure that if indeed there was any devil's play involved, Satan was dismayed to find me recommitting myself—with Christ's help—to embracing, surrendering to, and rejoicing in my love for God and God's abiding love for me.

After writing my letter to God and pledging to put our relationship first, I turned with a lighter heart to Psalm 138, my favorite:

I give you thanks, O Lord, with my whole heart;
Before the gods I sing your praise...
On the day I called, you answered me,
You increased my strength of soul.

The amazing, ridiculously improbable truth is that on the days I've called, God has answered me. And my strength of soul has increased. For that I give thanks with my whole, entire heart.

CHAPTER 10
sabbath discipline

"Be still and know that I am God."
–Psalm 46:10

PRACTICALLY SPEAKING, how do you put God first in the middle of a busy, modern life? Just the first step of making the commitment to prioritize my relationship with God had a transformative impact. My month-long malaise seemed to lift with a simple shift in cognition. It felt, much to my surprise, like it got me eighty percent of the way there. But what about the other twenty percent? How would I enact this intention in concrete ways? The opportunity to rise to the challenge came the very next day—Sunday. The Sabbath.

For over a year, as I began incorporating various Christian practices into my daily life, I had been observing the Sabbath. To my initial delight, I had experienced great success and spiritual richness in setting aside a full day each week for rest. Most notably, our family committed to honoring the Sabbath as a day without technology—no email, no Internet, no texting, no TV, no Facebook. It was refreshing, particularly in my relationship with my stepson Soren. In making a family rule of no media on Sunday, we could stop endlessly negotiating when and how much time he spent on the computer and on his cell phone. He knew they were off limits, and for some reason, he went along agreeably. We delighted in his company, spending newfound hours talking and laughing as a family, sitting on the back porch together without the pressure of to-do lists, errands, or any specific agenda.

But as my work life had increased in intensity in the subsequent months, I found my commitment slipping. I changed the "rules" and decided to end the Sabbath each week in the mid-afternoon, leaving the rest of the day and evening free to check email and respond to requests that had come in from coworkers over the weekend. After awhile, though, I started to question whether working on Sunday evenings really allowed me to honor the Sabbath properly and with fullness of heart. I realized that I spent most of Sunday with a small knot of anxiety in my stomach, anticipating the work hours ahead. This hardly seemed to support a goal of relaxing into a delight of God's creation by "lying fallow."

That afternoon, I asked myself: Could I wait until Monday morning to check email? My stomach clenched with a new anxiety. If I didn't go online, would I be perceived by coworkers as dropping the ball? *Would* I be dropping the ball? Would I be sacrificing some of my hard-won professional capital in a culture where all of my coworkers were online, all the time? Looking for advice, I texted my cousin John. In shorthand, I explained the dilemma. John is a devout Mormon and has a steadfast commitment to his Sabbath practice. Even while he was completing a competitive PhD program, knowing his classmates were working steadily throughout the weekend, he took off a full twenty-four hours from schoolwork every Sunday. Midnight to midnight. No exceptions. "Everyone on my team checks email Sunday night," I wrote him in my text. "So it's risky professionally. Feeling like I have to put God first, but scared for the consequences."

John's response came back within a few minutes. "Funny coincidence. Today was doing some meditating and thought of this scripture: Isaiah 58:13-14. Didn't know why until now. Perhaps God put it in my mind for you."

I turned to the passage, and the words of Isaiah sang to my heart:

If you refrain from trampling on the Sabbath,
From pursuing your own interests on my holy day;
If you call the Sabbath a delight and the holy day of the Lord honorable;
if you honor it, not going your own ways,
serving your own interests, or pursuing your own affairs;
then you shall take delight in the Lord,

and I will make you ride upon the heights of the earth;
I will feed you with the heritage of your ancestor Jacob,
for the mouth of the Lord has spoken.
(Isaiah 58:13-14)

I spend my life serving my own interests, putting my desires, ego, and needs first. But I had committed to a new approach: I was attempting to put God first. I had to admit that checking my email on Sundays was more about being perceived by my team as a "player"—and yes, I might sacrifice some professional capital if I didn't get online that night. But didn't I expect my new approach to involve some sacrifice? Reading the passage from Isaiah seemed to quell my anxiety; it was the answer I was seeking. The rest of the evening, spent in prayer, reading, and conversation, felt delicious and spacious.

Perhaps not surprisingly, my sleep is typically fitful on Sunday nights, prefaced by an evening of emails and anticipation of the demanding workweek ahead. But that night I slept deeply and woke up refreshed—feeling an eagerness to begin my week. In my new resolution to "put God first," it seemed like I was off to a good start.

Unfortunately, the sense of equanimity didn't last long.

CHAPTER 11

wild love

"Our best failures lie in the realm of parenting."
–Margaret Guenther, *The Practice of Prayer*

THERE IS NOTHING QUITE like the heart-compressing mixture of stress and guilt that comes with attempts to multi-task as a mother in the modern world. One afternoon later that week, I had set myself up. I needed to hustle Lila into the bath, take a quick shower myself, quickly reply to an urgent work email, finish packing a picnic dinner, and get us out the door where we'd meet Soren and his girlfriend at an outdoor music performance. All within thirty-five minutes. As we were leaving, I realized that our two cats had trapped a baby rabbit behind a bush, so we chased them around the yard until we caught them and saved the bunny. When we got to the performance site, there was no parking, and we circled futilely for almost twenty minutes until we found a spot, almost forty-five minutes late for the show. What pushed me to the edge, though, was that Lila kept up a non-stop monologue the entire time—during the bath, the emailing, the bunny chase, and the parking nightmare— full of endless observations, requests, instructions, and questions.

I was exhausted by the time we got home, and as I bustled Lila into bed, I snapped at her multiple times. She teared up. Not only were my nerves frayed, I was full of self-recrimination. I'd been doing so well in my first full week of trying to "put God first." Yet after just a few days, I'd already lost my equilibrium in a cloud of ill-tempered, frazzled stress. The stakes were higher than usual: I was bent on turning a new corner, determined not to backslide into the bleak, overwrought place I'd been in the months following Easter.

After I put Lila to bed, I sent up a silent prayer for help and picked up the book that had been on my bedside table. Reading through Margaret Guenther's chapter on parenting in *The Practice of Prayer* reassured and calmed me. "Since we are not God but flawed creatures, we inevitably fall short," Guenther writes. "Our children, who have experienced our love at its most generous and tender, also know us at our worst. They know our impatience and our resentments. They know the anger that we might be able to keep hidden from all others. They know our fallibility and our limitations. Most of the time they manage to love us anyway."

Indeed, we are not God. We are flawed. We are known in all of our limitations, and yet we are loved anyway. Our relationship with our children provides a small window into what God's love is like: boundless, forgiving, indelible. And the discipline of ending my day in silent prayer, after the multi-tasking madness, helped to stitch back my frayed nerves, soothing my spirit and helping me find and feel that love again.

The next day allowed for a fresh start, with tempers recalibrated and the irritability of the night before forgotten. That afternoon, I picked Lila up from camp and we drove around town doing errands. We started singing some of the repetitive, upbeat church songs we'd learned in Vacation Bible Camp earlier that summer. The mundane moment was suddenly transformed into something precious, memorable, and full of grace. Lila and I sang out at the top of our lungs with the car windows open, laughing, a joyful connection pulsing between us. "We sure are wild," my daughter said, grinning. Yes, we sure are wild. It's a wild love I have for my girl, a wild love I have for our God. Above all, it's a wild love that God has for us—chock full of abundant forgiveness. In classic call-and-response, Lila and I sang the words of the song, taking turns: "Let all God's people say 'Amen.'" "AMEN!" "Let all God's people say 'Amen.'" "AMEN!" "O praise the Lord!"

CHAPTER 12
downward mobility

"I fled Him, down the nights and
down the days;
I fled Him, down the arches of the years;
I fled Him, down the labyrinthine ways
Of my own mind; and in the midst of tears."
–Francis Thomas, *The Hound of Heaven*

AFTER MY CONVERSION, my mother-in-law gave me a book with Francis Thompson's famous poem, *The Hound of Heaven*. Thompson, whose opium and alcohol abuse left him destitute on the streets of London in the late 1800s, described how God pursued him through his years of addiction and non-belief. In the months after my baptism, I began to admit to myself the ways that I am plagued by a different type of addiction that constantly threatens to pull me away from God and that leaves me strung out with anxiety. It is what C.S. Lewis called the "great sin":

pride. It is an addiction to reputation, to praise, to a sense of self-worth based on external signs of accomplishment and social accolades. It leads to a competitiveness that creates an almost invisible yet undeniable backdrop in my life and permeates everyday interactions. I like to think that I hide it fairly well. Yet with quiet, often sideways approaches, I jockey for recognition and advancement. I know I'm not alone; this is common practice, particularly in the professional world and a fundamental part of our culture. Yet as the first-born child of high-achieving parents and as a transplant to the South from an ultra-competitive community in the Northeast, this demon seems to nip at my heels more frequently than it does for others I know.

This struggle became exacerbated as I left graduate school. I applied for jobs feeling like my assignment was to "make something of myself." Henri Nouwen describes this as the "temptation to be spectacular." A subtle but pervasive uneasiness settled in because I wasn't sure how to manifest a spectacular career. Unlike studying hard and getting good grades, making something of myself out in the real world—presumably by gaining status, power, and relevance—was at least partly out of my control. And I generally liked things I could control.

In the months after my baptism, I began to question the way I was approaching my work life. The restless, uneasy ambition and biting insecurity were taking their toll; I felt increasingly exhausted. I wondered how could I give up the stress but keep the drive—which included many valuable elements such as engagement and enthusiasm. How could I avoid the painful roller coaster of trying to "get ahead" which meant that every meeting and every encounter with coworkers became a chance to try to prove myself?

In reading scripture, I began to understand the ways in which Christianity provides a profoundly different roadmap of how to live. Jesus said, "Whoever wishes to be great among you must be your servant and whoever wishes to be first among you must be your slave; just as the Son of Man came not to be served but to serve" (Matthew 20:26-28). Instead of trying to position myself to rise to the top, the spiritual path involves a very different assignment in two parts. The first part of the mandate is to say yes to God's call, which includes saying yes to the gifts I've been given and having an honest acceptance of my limitations. At the same time, as Christ's disciple, I have to abandon what Nouwen describes as the "way of upward mobility in which our world has invested so much." Instead, I must embrace a "downward mobility ending on the cross."

As this central principle of Christianity started to sink in, part of me responded with panic. What had I signed up for? Weren't prestige and accomplishment the source of my value? Wouldn't a slow but steady climb upward be the thing that would generate admiration from friends and coworkers? The thing that would lead my mother to tell proud stories about me to her friends?

At the same time, I found that Jesus' teachings came as a huge relief. His command translates into accountability and liberation at the same time. It means that I can't retreat from my vocational calling out of fear or laziness. I can't stay home in my sweatpants with my remote control when things get tough. If I did, I wouldn't be honoring God's creation in me. But neither can I exhaust myself with the relentless anxiety of ambition for its own sake. Rather, I have to focus on responding to the ways I'm called to serve others with love—not just the poor or marginalized, but also my coworkers, my family, and my community.

If I did that, I assumed the rest would take care of itself.

* * *

"Lauren, I'd like you to go to New York with us. It's time to really put the spotlight on you."

We were in a meeting at work. Lauren is a colleague whom I like and admire but who is also a natural competitor. We have similar skills, fill an overlapping niche on the team, and work closely together on projects. There was a high-level, high-status meeting coming up, and she was being asked by our director to travel to make a presentation on behalf of our group. This was a big deal—a real opportunity for visibility and advancement. I had not been invited. It didn't appear that I had even been considered.

How do you practice "downward mobility" in practical terms? How do you stay oriented toward love and manifest it in tangible ways, especially in a hierarchical, secular, fast-paced, data-driven work environment? When Lauren was chosen to present at the meeting, my stomach clenched in automatic jealousy like a well-trained muscle. I could feel how easy it would be to slip into a funk of resentment, or worse, to undermine her in small but substantial ways.

I wanted to take a different approach. I wanted to strengthen a new, underused muscle. A muscle that—if I could shake off the atrophy and limber it up—would allow me to live out Christ's command to love my neighbor more fully in body and spirit. So I prayed about it. I asked how I could honor and celebrate my colleague. Over the next few weeks, I cultivated compassion and affection for her in my prayers and dwelled in the realization that I wanted her to be happy. Sure enough, I observed my jealously shift as a feeling of love for her grew. I knew the New York meeting was a great chance for her to shine and that she certainly deserved it after years of hard work on our team. And so I made a conscious decision that I would be her ally all the way.

Then I asked: what does being her ally look and feel like? I realized the best way I could serve her would be to step back. Rather than jumping in to try to be "helpful" as she prepared for the meeting—which would just be a subtle attempt to exalt myself by seeking to gain attention from our leadership group—I hung back. I reviewed her materials when she asked me to, but I stayed firmly on the sidelines.

A few weeks later, I observed part of the New York meeting by videoconference. Lauren did a fabulous job. Amazingly, I felt peaceful and happy about it; the hounds of jealousy and anxiety weren't biting at my heels. Perhaps it was an indication that I'd done something right as I shifted my inner stance and slowly, in a small way, enjoyed a taste of what it feels like to love my neighbor as myself.

The next chance to practice "downward mobility" came almost immediately. A week later I traveled to Boston to visit my parents and bumped into an old college friend. Daniel is an up-and-coming writer, with essays published in national magazines and a recent book deal with a well-known publisher. He had heard from a mutual friend that I had recently been baptized. Standing on the street corner, he told me that he had recently had a spiritual conversion experience himself. He said he was nervous to tell people and hesitant to write about the experience, assuming that both his community and his readers would be turned off by his new-found religiosity. I told him I'd been doing some writing about my spiritual journey. Would he be interested in reading a few of my essays? Yes, he'd love to see them. I left our encounter gripping a scrap of paper with his email address.

I spent the next week struggling with my demons. The "temptation to be spectacular" reared its ugly head. I had fantasies that Daniel might react to my writing with astonishment, telling me it could lead to Something Big. His imagined praise would serve as validation that I ought to stick with the project. Maybe he'd refer me to an agent, or at the very least, insist that I pursue publication. How quickly my restless, ambitious monkey-mind spun out of control.

I knew all of this was dangerous territory. Yet when I got quiet, I also felt a compelling inner "nudge" to send Daniel the early draft of my writing. I hadn't been expecting to bump into him, and our meeting didn't feel accidental. I was starting to trust this inner impulse, but in this instance, I figured I should disregard the nudge because clearly my ego was wrapped tightly around this idea of sharing my writing. No good could come of that.

In the days ahead, however, through prayer and reflection, I realized I could have a different orientation to engaging my friend. He had revealed his own vulnerability and insecurity around writing about his spiritual journey. Instead of sending him my draft as a way to exalt myself or seek validation, could I see it as a kind of ministry? Could it become an opportunity to provide him with encouragement, support, and friendship—without expecting anything except perhaps his companionship in return? As I prayed about it, I could feel my intention shifting. The "temptation to be spectacular" seemed to melt away. I sensed that somehow, in a way that was not altogether clear to me, I might be serving him and our friendship by sharing my writing. In my prayers, the nudge remained strong, and so I sent it off. The end result was the same, but remarkably, my inner orientation had completely changed.

Jesus calls us to serve, not to seek to be served. His command requires a shift in me that is so fundamental, so monumental, it must occur almost at the cellular level. So perhaps it is no surprise that the progress I made didn't last long. I found myself backsliding almost immediately. It turned out that Daniel didn't have a dramatic reaction to my writing either way. He emailed me back a warm but brief note a few weeks later, offering me a few pieces of constructive feedback. The hounds immediately returned, howling with indignation at his lackluster response. My pious motivation disappeared so fast I had whiplash. The ugly truth was undeniable: I wanted to be spectacular! And I wanted to use Daniel and our relationship to help me get there.

In the months after my baptism, I found I was constantly confronted with opportunities to slip back into old habits, to embrace competitiveness and self-promotion in subtle but undeniable ways, to take refuge in advancement instead of communion. In these moments, I realized the extent to which I was only at the beginning of my spiritual conversion. And I knew that without help, there was no way I could make the colossal change that Jesus' mandate requires. I couldn't do it on my own. I would have to turn myself fully over to God's care and command.

I just wasn't sure exactly what that involved.

KATE H. RADEMACHER

PART 4

learning to surrender

CHAPTER 13
what moves me most

"When he was in the house he asked them,
'What were you arguing about on the way?'
But they were silent, for on the way they had
argued with one another who was the greatest.
He sat down, called the twelve, and said to
them, 'Whoever wants to be first must be last
of all and servant of all.'"
–Mark 9:33-35

ONE DAY I TURNED to the gospel of Mark during my morning prayers and read of how the disciples had argued with one another about who was the greatest among them. I mentioned the passage to David over breakfast, and he quipped, "Sounds like you and your family when you're playing cards."

I continued to notice all the ways I struggled with ego and competitiveness, not just when playing games on vacation with my parents and brothers, but as a pervasive part of everyday interactions. That morning, I proceeded with my day and forgot about the morning's scriptural passage. Later that night, I needed to finish up some work after I put Lila to bed. As part of my attempt to put my relationship with God first in small, everyday ways—and to avoid ending up as a spiritually-bereft devotee of the professional grind—I had recently made a commitment to set aside a brief time for prayer on those evenings when I needed to work, before booting up my computer and delving into email.

In doing so that evening, I felt something new and unexpected in my prayers. Within just a few minutes of sitting down and getting quiet, I felt as if an invisible hand was pushing on my neck and shoulders, a great heaviness that was an internal sensation but nevertheless distinct and palpable. I'd never experienced this before. I bowed my head further, feeling as though the Spirit's hand was urging me downward. I was confused, unsure of the meaning.

When I opened my email account, there was a note from our communications department at the top of my Inbox. The publication I had been working on feverishly for two weeks was ready to go out. But they recommended that rather than listing my name as a co-author, it would be better to just have one author listed—the senior director of our group—in order to have a more clear, unified public presence for our organization. The disappointment I felt was immediate and sharp. I had worked on this project over weekends and on a paid holiday. I had been motivated by many things including—there was no denying it—the knowledge that this was a high-profile project that would come with public recognition and kudos.

I sat there, stunned, contemplating my next move. I thought also of the heavy hand of pressure I'd felt in my prayers just moments before. And then, the memory of that morning's scriptural passage came to me: "Whoever wants to be first must be last of all and servant of all."

The meaning was clear. It was another reminder that all my maneuvering to be great, to seek advancement, was misguided. As Christ's disciple, I am here to serve. I returned to prayer, contemplating how to transform myself into a servant in this situation. The truth is that I have incredible respect for the director; she's a fabulous, intelligent leader. The topic we were writing about was a critical public health issue that we had the opportunity to elevate in an important online forum. After twenty minutes of contemplation and asking for God's help, my attitude shifted. I found I could let go of my attachment to credit and could celebrate the project moving forward without my name attached. I wasn't a saint. Entrails of disappointment remained, but they were greatly diminished. It felt good—even joyful—to transform my attitude into one of service.

But a few minutes later, my boss called. She had seen the email and insisted that I remain listed on the publication as a contributor. I quickly ping-ponged back, asserting that it was all right; our senior director should be the one. Surprised, I realized I really meant it. Yet my boss was adamant that I share the recognition. She got off the phone and wrote an email to the team insisting that my name remain. Her advice was accepted, and the decision was reversed.

Here was another twist. Out of it, more questions arose: How does one receive accolades and advancement with a spiritually-pure heart? Is it possible? If one's reputation is stripped away, perhaps it is more straightforward to assume the persona of a servant. Just be loving and help out; no thanks required. But what if one is offered back the temptation of esteem and success? How can one remain a servant then?

The implied message in my boss' phone call was that the recognition I would receive from having my name on the publication would help give my voice legitimacy and influence in the public arena. Could that, in turn, help me better serve others? I wondered if getting credit could be not about jockeying to be great but rather become a way to honor God and to honor my role as a co-pilot in navigating my life story with God. To recognize God at the helm with me actively manifesting the work God calls me to do in this world. I realized that perhaps the point is not to eschew reputation entirely. If recognition and status could open doors that would help me serve others and live more fully into God's calling for me, then I figured it generally passed spiritual muster.

Yet this also seemed like precarious ground given the endless temptation to yank back control, to try to grasp at one's own greatness. In Paul's letter to the Galatians, he poses key questions we must continually ask ourselves: "Am I now seeking the favor of men, or of God? Or am I trying to please men? If I were still pleasing men, I should not be a servant of Christ" (Galatians 1:10). These questions seem to be good touchstones in everyday life. There are many people to serve: my family, my co-workers, my community. And it is good to please them, but the real, important question is: Do my actions glorify and please God?

* * *

It is one thing to have an intellectual understanding that God is at the helm of one's life, but it's something else altogether to feel the truth of it in your body and spirit. As I continued to seek guidance in prayer about how to radically reorient my worldview and actions, I began to have moments of awareness of what it actually means to do this: to let go, to trust, to give up control.

When I was a little girl, my father taught me to dance. He was a master at the jitterbug. He would swing me around the living room, changing directions quickly with elaborate footwork, first pulling me close so that we were cheek-to-cheek then pushing me out in a complicated spin. With my hand in his, feeling the rhythm of the music and his subtle changes in direction, I learned to follow his lead. Never knowing where he'd move next, I discovered how to listen with my body.

Now, I was learning a new dance. I realized if I could listen in a new way, I could let God take over with a silent, barely perceptible guiding hand. With me unsteady at first—taking the stumbling, jerky steps of a beginner. But then, with increasing fluidity, I learned to release into the embrace, waiting for the next silent cue.

The 14th century Christian writer Thomas á Kempis creates a dialogue between Christ and the reader in his book *The Imitation of Christ* in which Christ instructs us to "consider whether it be My honor or self-interest that moves you most." What moves me most? The truth is, I am pitifully inept at orienting my movements by any compass other than self-interest. To learn to do otherwise is the discipline of a lifetime. Thankfully, through God's grace and help, I was at least beginning to recognize the beauty and glory that come from following God's lead, rather than trying to grab for control and, in turn, tripping over my own ego and pride.

What moves me most? The sirens of praise, recognition, reputation, promotion? No, what moves me most is when I *can* let go and feel God's almost imperceptible hand on my back, quietly guiding me on the next step forward. Endless temptation will remain to do otherwise, yet I realize that this is the dance to which I wanted to devote my life.

CHAPTER 14

a chosen love

"When he came to the place where the wild
things are, they roared their terrible roars and
gnashed their terrible teeth and rolled their
terrible eyes and showed their terrible claws."

–Maurice Sendak, *Where the Wild Things Are*

ON SOME DAYS, I thought I was starting to make progress
in learning to follow God's lead. But at home and in my
marriage, I felt like one of the wild things in Maurice
Sendak's classic children's book, roaring a terrible roar
and gnashing my teeth. Sometimes I did this silently and
internally, other times with demanding tears and through
fervent negotiations. In the months following my prayer
experience by the lake in Vermont—when the vivid image
of a curly-haired, would-be son appeared—my hunger
for another baby had abated somewhat. I was appeased
temporarily by the idea that perhaps *not* having another

biological baby was part of God's plan for me. But then the restless ache crept back into my heart. The desire for another child that was so strong I could feel it in the back of my throat and in the roof on my mouth. Driving around town, I would glance through windows at babies strapped into their car seats and begin weeping without any warning, my vision blurred as I maneuvered my way through traffic.

So the negotiations with David started up again. I cajoled, listened, debated, cried. I would make commitments to myself and to David to move on, to let go of the drama and discontent. Then within days, I would lose my resolve again.

During that time, David turned fifty. I recognized that despite what they say about fifty being the new forty, it is a hard age to start over, especially when life was full with two kids—one from each of two marriages—busy careers, a hectic social calendar, and rich spiritual lives. Yet at age thirty-four, I felt underutilized; I had a deep sense that I had more mothering to do. And so I gnashed my teeth, rolled my eyes. There was a wild thing in me that wouldn't be satiated.

At one point in Sendak's story, Max stills the beasts with a single word: "No." No is a hard word. As a well-off, well-educated American in the 21st century, I was taught that the options are limitless, that I can "have it all." Thus, the "no" I experienced on the baby issue came as an even more surprising and bitter pill. In my case, the "no" came in different shapes. Certainly, it came through David's voice—clear and unwavering after his own long process of discernment. And it was painful for him. In bed one day, as I curled my body around his, he said softly, "You know, it's really hard to disappoint you and make you mad for years. If the roles were reversed, this would be incredibly hard on you."

I appreciated the impact on him. Yet even though I knew it was hurting him and our marriage, I found myself clinging to the anger and disappointment, unwilling for some reason to let it go. A friend helped me see the ongoing angst in a new light. "God's gonna trouble the waters," she said simply after listening to my latest litany of frustrations about the issue. "Perhaps the agitated waters are a sign that God isn't done yet."

With that possibility in mind, I turned back to prayer. I asked God if it was really God's will that I not have another biological baby. *Yes*, I felt in response. But what am I to do with all this longing and agitation in my heart? The answer came back: *Focus on Soren*.

* * *

On Mother's Day that year, I had come downstairs in the morning to find a card from my seventeen-year-old stepson propped on the mantle. Soren was still asleep; he rarely emerged from his cave-like bedroom on the weekends until the early afternoon. Curious about the card and not wanting to wait several hours to read it, I took a peek.

"Happy Mother's Day! You know, you really are my mother. Despite your special title of stepmother, you have put in the time and you are my mother. I was thinking today that you really have influenced my life and my personality. You aren't a third party. You are part of what makes me up. I have none of your genes but much of who I am is rooted in what I have learned from you. I think I am just as much the product of you as I am of my other parents."

My heart did a double take. How did I get here? How did I arrive at this blessed place of having a son—not of my flesh but of my heart—claiming me as his parent?

Soren was four when his father and I started dating. He and I became buddies fast. Building a hut out of debris in the woods, we dubbed it the "fart fort," giggling and writing a song to the tune of "Yellow Submarine" about the adventures we'd have. Admittedly, my situation was helped by a key factor that is not typical for most people I know who are dating or married to someone with children from a prior marriage: Soren's mother was sane, warm and—remarkably—not threatened by my entrance onto the scene. Her divorce from David was without any major contention or drama. I couldn't relate to their easy parting of ways; most break-ups I'd had involved wrenching months of tears and jealous betrayals or desperate, late-night, take-me-back negotiations. But with Soren's mom, it was different. When I married Soren's dad, she attended our wedding and gave us her blessing. It made a huge difference as I navigated my new role as wife and stepmother.

In the years after the wedding, my attitude was that I occupied a separate and unique place in Soren's life, and it was important for me not to overstep my bounds. Soren had a perfectly good dad and mom, and it wasn't appropriate or necessary for me to try to be a second mother. At times, David pushed me to assume a parenting role out of his desire for a cozy family experience, but I resisted. Partly, it felt like there would be too many cooks in the kitchen. But more than that, there remained a perceptible and respectful distance between Soren and me. While Soren would curl his body into David's lap— clearly belonging to him in a deep, flesh-from-flesh kind of way—I never had that kind of intimacy with him. One night when David was called away to an evening meeting, I put Soren to bed, a ritual that usually took over an hour. Somewhat awkwardly, I started to sing his favorite lullaby an octave higher than his dad typically sang it. After a few lines, we both laughed nervously. It didn't feel right. The sleepy tenderness of the evening was special, but I was a caretaker in that moment, not a parent.

In some ways, this semi-distant role was convenient. I could pop in and out of the never-ending river of decisions, tasks, and chores related to raising a child— attending a teacher conference occasionally or preparing a snack once in awhile. I didn't have the same day-in day-out, bottom line, where's-my-kid-now, you-depend-on-me relationship with him. When Lila was born, I realized that this dependency was the thing that made parenting so demanding but also so rewarding. Never getting a break, always being accountable to another human was often draining. But through some special alchemy, it also made my heart ache with unending, unquenchable love. My daughter and I owned each other. While Soren and I liked and even loved each other, we didn't own one another in quite the same way.

As the years passed and Soren entered adolescence, though, I felt a desire to be more and to do more for him. I found myself more and more in the role of rule-setter, advocate, worrywart, advisor, and even decision-maker. I explained to a friend over coffee how I had always kept my distance, staying carefully in my place in the "other" category when it came to parenting. But over time, things had been slowly changing. "You know," she said, taking a sip of her tea and looking at me carefully, "when you describe your relationship with Soren, it sure sounds like you're a full-fledged parent." Her comment startled me. Was it true? Was it time for a shift? As I reflected on it more, I felt a growing certainty inside me; I wanted to parent Soren more fully. I wanted to claim him as my child.

Eager to act on this desire but worried about overstepping my bounds, I initiated conversations with both David and Soren's mom about my intention to step up more into the role of parent. They both looked at me with blank, "Where have you been?" stares. My claiming to be one of Soren's parents came as no surprise to them; they felt as though I'd been in that role for years.

The difference this new intention made in my interactions with Soren was both subtle and concrete. I took more accountability and engaged more deeply. I arranged to have Soren see a new learning disabilities specialist and helped organize a summer internship for him at a nearby college. I nagged him more frequently and hugged him more often. The card he left for me on Mother's Day confirmed the change I felt in our relationship. We had made our claims on each other.

So why, six months after I had made this shift, was God telling me in my prayers to re-focus my attention on Soren? Hadn't God been paying attention?

Despite our closeness, Soren and I are opposites in many ways. He moves through life slowly and distractedly, burdened by Attention Deficit Disorder, while I catapult through life at full and often anxious speeds. The truth was, after several weeks of increasing frustration as he floundered at school, despite all of his dad's and my best efforts to help, I was ready to distance myself again. We were in a rough patch, and although it wasn't a conscious choice, I realized I was poised to opt out and let his dad, as the "real parent," continue to sweat it out. But apparently, that was not God's will for me.

Throughout this time, I had been asking God for guidance in dealing with my ongoing anger and disappointment about not getting to have another biological baby. One week during the Eucharist, I prayed for help with the baby dilemma and with knowing how best to parent Soren. In our church, the homemade communion bread is baked with a lot of honey. As the intense flavor spread over my tongue, my taste buds reminded me of the sweetness that comes from following God's lead. We suffer through the "no's" in our life. The wild beasts of longing in our hearts gnash their teeth, show their claws, and roar their roars. But as Thomas Merton writes in *New Seeds of Contemplation*, "The man...who lets God lead him peacefully through the wilderness...will taste the peace and joy of union with God."

God seemed to be calling me to learn what it means to be a parent by choice, rather than just a parent of flesh. Truly, God always allows us choice. In our creation, we were given freedom, and we can choose to love, to distance, to connect, or to reject. God chooses us, but does not force us to love God any more than we are forced to love our neighbor. This freedom is an incredible gift, but also leaves the window open to opt out at any time, often through passivity, busyness, or sheer distraction. A love without coercion has the potential to be fully actualized, but loving by choice takes intention, patience, and perseverance. Maybe that's why God kept troubling my waters, so that I gained the opportunity to understand more fully what chosen love really is and can become.

After feeling God's nudge in my prayers, I opted back in. The shift resulted in small, but meaningful changes in my interactions with Soren. I helped him edit his college essay. I made him lunch one day when he was late for school, even though we had an agreement that he would make it himself. Later that evening, as I watched him leaning against the kitchen counter, laughing, I felt a big, heart-constricting love for him. It was an entirely different feeling from the respectful fondness I'd experienced in the past. In all my years of wanting another baby, I had been longing for more of the intensity of a love that comes from mutually belonging to another person. That evening, after I listened to Soren vent about a frustration at school, he grabbed me into a quick sideways hug. "Thanks for listening," he said. "It made a big difference." Yes, opening one's heart and choosing love does make a difference. It makes all the difference.

CHAPTER 15
forgiveness

"May you hear from heaven, your dwelling
place, forgive and render to all whose heart
know you, according to all their ways, for only
you know the human heart."
—2 Chronicles 6:30

DESPITE THE GIFT of my deepening relationship with
Soren, I still couldn't shake the low-grade, persistent anger
that had become an increasingly significant part of my
relationship with David. I *was* grateful for the beautiful
life we had built together, and I felt guilty for not being
able to move on. But despite all my prayerful efforts, I just
couldn't accept that I hadn't gotten my way in manifesting
all of what I wanted: a big, hectic family with lots of kids
and with all the chaos and love that comes with it. Instead
we had something else which certainly was remarkably
sweet—a peaceful family scene in which there was space

for us to lie together reading quietly on a rainy Sunday. There were no infants or toddlers to spoon-feed mashed bananas, no one to chase and pin down in an attempt to change a dirty diaper. Soren was getting ready to depart for college, and it was a small family that would remain behind, but one full of connection and beauty.

And so it was confusing to feel a flush of gratitude and the pinch of anger and disappointment in my marriage all at once. I realized that perhaps this is the pinch of all adulthood. I was feeling it at just about the right time as I reached my mid-thirties. With the open-ended possibilities of young adulthood behind, there was a natural taking-stock calculation of both the blessings and limitations in one's unique path. Of course, it is always possible to redirect the course of one's life, even up until the moment of death. Still, there is an important accounting one does, not just of the remaining possibilities and ambitions, but also of the limitations and boundaries that contain us.

So even as David and I continued to share tremendous closeness and tenderness, my anger was always hovering in the background, like a low-grade headache. He was patient and understanding, but my chronic disappointment became increasingly exhausting for both of us. What does one do with this type of anger, I wondered, especially when it's directed toward the one you've signed up to cherish through marriage?

This is a question that many of us ask ourselves as we consider the lives we have and the lives we're creating. As I sought the answer, I looked at the friend whose husband was diagnosed with a serious but curable illness. His treatment required lengthy, invasive interventions that left him perpetually grouchy, distant, and exhausted for several years. Or another friend whose husband deals with chronic underemployment; he can't seem to land or keep a steady job. Or another whose wife's mismanagement of a work deadline meant they missed a planned family trip to his childhood home. It turned out it would have been his last opportunity to see his mother; she passed away unexpectedly that month. Forgiveness is needed not just for these bigger resentments but even for the small slights and disappointments that can build up in a cumulative plaque on a marriage's gum line. Forgiveness is required even for things that don't involve any wrongdoing or fault but are just the realities of life. There were days when I felt disappointed that as I was delighting in the thrill of my conversion journey, David was devotedly rooted in another faith. While he and I could enjoy tennis match conversations about spiritual concepts, there was little we could do by way of sharing worship or ritual.

And I knew there were dozens of ways that I disappointed and angered David, not least of which was my inability to find resolution about an issue that should have already been settled between us.

We are told, but we don't quite comprehend at the outset, the ways that marriage will disappoint as well as fulfill us, the ways in which asking for and offering forgiveness for minor and major disappointments must become a necessary routine. The Christian path tells us that to do otherwise—to create or perpetuate brokenness in relationships or to allow disconnection to become the status quo—is a sin.

For most of my life, I had practiced small, everyday acts of forgiveness, but I hadn't needed to dig into the deeper challenge of forgiveness as a spiritual practice. When I was honest with myself, I wasn't sure what that involved or, even, what forgiveness really means. The Lord's Prayer offers help. It is a ubiquitous part of Christian life and worship, and through it we regularly ask for God's forgiveness while at the same time, we commit to forgiving others. Jesus' postscript to the Lord's Prayer in Matthew's gospel illuminates the magnitude of this practice: "For if you forgive others their trespasses, your heavenly Father will also forgive you; but if you do not forgive others, neither will your Father forgive your trespasses" (Matthew 6:14). This is not so much a quid-pro-quo, but speaks to the circular nature of forgiving and forgiveness. God calls us into a covenant of relationship—with God and with each other. Sin is a breaking of this commitment to remain in relationship. And forgiveness is reaching across the chasm to form a bridge back to some kind of wholeness. Not denying the crevices or what caused them, but loving through them and despite them.

When this is challenging, scripture goes on to reassure us that "love is patient" (1 Corinthians 13: 4). The process of forgiving and forgiveness requires patience as well. A church in my community was rocked with scandal when the treasurer embezzled almost half a million dollars. In the church newsletter, the priest of the large congregation wrote, "I'm at a place where I want to be able, to want to be able, to want to be able to forgive." I realized I should not condemn myself when I do not start off (or even end up) manifesting forgiveness perfectly. But to more in that direction, even if slowly, haltingly, this is the task.

A friend who dealt with a major betrayal in her marriage—eleven months of secret infidelity—and then a decision to get divorced, finally found forgiveness through a daily practice of prayer and meditation in which she imagined her anger sitting beside her, hunkered down as a separate, dark entity. She accepted its presence but saw it as distinct from her. She didn't overly identify with it. She did this for many, many months. She knew she was getting better on the day that the dark presence got up and left in the middle of one her meditations. You can't rush anger, but you can practice patience while you wait for the hunkering mass to move on.

God gave us emotions and so expects us to feel them, to accept them, and to pay attention to their meaning in our lives. To deny or push away our feelings is to deny part of God's creation. But to accept and welcome our emotions can be hard. Anger can feel like a scary thing; it was generally unwelcome in my family growing up. But one day in prayer, after a series of common annoyances at the breakfast table, the pump was primed. After the dishes were cleared and the kids hustled off to school, I brought all of the anger I had been experiencing to my morning prayer. It was silver hot, fully experienced in my body and psyche.

And in response, I sensed that God was relaxed about it all, entirely willing for me to bring the intensity to our encounter. I was also aware of something else—that just beyond the boundaries of my anger, God dwelled in perfect, complete, and utter stillness. There was a well of peace available through God that I could access at any time. It was my choice. I could cross that boundary and enter the empty and divine quiet. I could stay with the silver heat. Both were okay with God; there wasn't any shame, demand, or rush. Just an open invitation.

CHAPTER 16
taking it up with God

"As he was setting out on a journey, a man
ran up and knelt before him, and asked him,
'Good Teacher, what must I do to inherit
eternal life?' Jesus said to him…'You know the
commandments….' He said to him, 'Teacher,
I have kept all these since my youth.' Jesus,
looking at him, loved him and said, 'You lack
one thing; go, sell what you own, and give the
money to the poor, and you will have treasure
in heaven; then come, follow me.' When he
heard this, he was shocked and went away
grieving, for he had many possessions."

–Mark 10: 17-22

I WASN'T READY. Despite the invitation that I felt from God
in my prayers, and even though I was tired of the morass
in my own head and heart, I found I wasn't ready to give
up my anger. As I continued to seek resolution, David and

118

I began to explore a new idea: the possibility of becoming foster parents. David was clear that he couldn't take on the life-long commitment of parenting another child, but what if we offered to care for a kid that needed a safe home on a temporary basis?

I felt uncertain about the idea. It seemed like an uneasy compromise between us, and I was fearful that fostering a child with a chaotic family situation and history of abuse or neglect could turn our lives upside down.

One weekend I went hiking in the woods, mind restless, hungry for answers. Murmuring a prayer as I walked, I came upon an enormous, thick-trunked tree, stretching to the sky, ram-rod straight. Beside it was a tiny sapling with only a few leaves on its spindly branches. The small tree clearly was not thriving, perhaps even dying. Standing beside the two trees, I suddenly felt God's answer to the question that David and I had been considering. Our family, I recognized, was like the big tree: strong, stable, and loving enough to welcome, nurture, and shelter a hurting child beneath our branches.

Still, I was uncertain if I'd gotten the message right. As I sat in silence one morning a few weeks later, asking for help, an internal vision of God emerged, holding out a child. The image was foggy in my mind's eye, but the promise was not. There would be another child in my life. Not a biological baby. But somehow—perhaps in a totally unexpected and unplanned way—a child would come. I opened my Bible to a page at random, and the words were searing: "Take heed now, for the Lord has chosen you to build a house as the sanctuary; be strong and act." (1 Chronicles, 28: 10)

With this sense of promise and command, one might have expected that I would embrace this new vision with a joyful, accepting heart. Instead, my fear, grief, and anger intensified. I was reminded of the rich man described in Mark's gospel. He enjoys a certain celebrity status because Jesus gave him one of the most challenging and confusing commands that haunts Christians even today. He was told to give away all of his money to the poor. Not some, or even a lot. No, Jesus told him to give it *all* away. He was a good man who obeyed all of the commandments his entire life, but both he and God knew that something was still missing. So he asked Jesus what else he had to do, and he received a startling answer: Give your money away and follow me.

What strikes me about this exchange is not so much the content of the message but the rich man's reaction. He had been hungry for God his whole life, so much so that he committed to a rigorous spiritual path for years. And even after all that time, he yearned for more. Then, amazingly, he got to see God face-to-face. He didn't have to contend with the messy, slow process of discernment. He got to hear Christ's command with his own ears. But despite all this, when the next steps were laid out concretely before him, was he happy? Was he relieved? No. Instead scripture tells us that "he was shocked and went away grieving." (Mark: 9:22)

Shocked, grieving? These don't sound like words that describe a person who just received crystal clear guidance on how to realize his wildest dreams: Just do one fairly straightforward thing and he's there. I realized that this reaction of shock and grief is how it can be for all of us. We crave God's direction, straining our ears to hear the quiet sighs and whispers of the Spirit. But then, when the answer comes, the initial reaction is not always relief, peace, and joy. Instead, we go away grieving. Or, in my case, I often go kicking and screaming.

What God asks of us can be incredibly hard. We know this, of course, from Christ's own example in his journey to the cross. But we don't necessarily expect or accept our feelings of anger, confusion, resentment, or sadness when we are asked to follow God's lead. When the call comes, I would prefer a swell of orchestral music and a warm, joyful certainty that fills my heart like a melted chocolate bar. I crave a clarity and trust that don't dwindle or leave any room for doubt or grief or anger. I can practically see that rich man, leaning against the wall with his arms crossed at a jaunty angle, winking at me: "Yeah right. Dream on."

I decided to lay out the confusing tangle at Christ's feet with the hope that he would help me. Help me to release the ironclad grip on my anger and confusion and cross over into that place of peace that God always offers up. In my prayers, I imagined my anger and fear as a modern art sculpture, an ugly, overworked monstrosity. It had a lemon in the center, with strands of barbed wire sticking out and curling around in a softball-sized orb. Luckily, the ugly thing didn't take up much of the space inside me—only a small section on the display shelf. The rest was filled with non-offensive, pastel watercolor landscapes and pretty vases of still-life flowers. Still, that bulbous eyesore seemed to be on permanent display.

Until one Sunday during church. As I knelt in prayer, I was surprised to feel Jesus grab the ugly thing and hurl it away. I felt him then settling in me, promising to fill up the gap—the empty space that remained behind. I was pleased. But moments later as I turned the corner to return to my pew after the Eucharist, there was a friend's cute two-year-old kid, and I was back to coveting my neighbor's bounty. As I kneeled, Jesus appeared again in my prayerful imagination. He tossed the anger away a second time and settled back without fanfare. An hour or so later, I revisited the image of the bulging lemon sculpture, and found that Jesus was cradling the persistent, pokey mess like a newborn baby. Is this what it's all about? God alternatively cradling and chucking away our tangled web of suffering and uncertainty—patiently and as many times as it takes? Offering to fill the gap with divine love?

* * *

A friend of mine warns that "grace" is an overused word, but what word better describes the experience of the switch being flipped when the anger I'd been holding onto so tightly for so many years finally started to dissipate? I don't know if this shift happened because I had invited Jesus in to help, or if God just decided it was time.

The soul-sagging relief came from adopting a new strategy. I decided to take the issue up with God, instead of taking it up with David. I remembered that my job is to surrender—again and again—to God's direction and will.

The relief came in realizing that there was no problem. I felt called to nurture another child; God was offering me a path forward. We could become foster parents. It wouldn't be the same as having a biological baby, but maybe this was God's will for us. David was on-board; he was willing to give this crazy thing a try together. We agreed that we'd wait until Soren left for college and then sign up to take the required eight-week class offered by the Department of Social Services, at least to check it out. But even beyond these concrete action steps, there was suddenly a whole new and obvious game plan: Let go of my grasping ways and hand myself over to God. In finally feeling a faith in God's will and promise for me, the thrashing attempts to wrestle life's outcomes to fit my own agenda quieted; my heart and mind became still. And it didn't just feel good, it felt great.

I was suddenly like one of those five thousand, lined up patiently, waiting for the basket to be passed with a morsel of Christ's fish and loaves of bread, with the promise that it would satisfy. I found a glimmer of trust that something wild, unexpected, and perhaps even miraculous would happen. The outcome wouldn't be something I could control; the path might challenge me in ways I couldn't foresee.

I also knew God might change the plan midcourse. On the day Jesus fed the five thousand, he'd originally set out for a "lonely place" (Mark 6:30). But the crowds followed him—and either he changed the plan or he accepted the new direction as the day unfolded. While practicing faith means holding out for God's promise, it certainly does not mean trying to hold God rigidly accountable to my perception of what the promise might mean. Instead it is surrendering to the fog of the unknown and trusting God's lead despite my fears, despite my desire for immediate answers and resolution, despite the discomfort that lingers. The relief comes in placing myself—over and over again—in God's open palms.

After a sermon at church that Sunday, Lila tucked a note into my lap, full of misspellings as well as profound truth: "You cane let gowe of you self and let god yoos you. Rfus—no!" The translation: "You can let go of yourself and let God use you. Refuse? No!" It is a mistake to think that the litmus test for whether God's call is legitimate is that we feel one hundred percent comfortable with the plan at the outset. But when we do get on board, there is nothing quite like the peace that replaces the fear, uncertainty, and resistance. So, as Lila's note advised, I cannot refuse. I can only surrender and let God use me.

When I'm tempted to let the flush of disappointment rise up like bile in my throat, I turn back to that. "This is between you and me, God." It's a new mantra. Perhaps this is where we should always start when we seek forgiveness in marriage or in other relationships: by taking it up with God. When we're angered by those closest to us—resentful of their sickness, their distraction, their lack of appreciation, their differences, the limitations and betrayals—we can first ask God if and how these challenges somehow hold our next assignment in their midst. Rather than pouring all of our agitation into expecting that the other person should change, we can ask God to help transform our minds and hearts, with the knowledge that the ripple effects of that transformation can and will take many forms. By turning to God and releasing ourselves into God's care, we are able to linger for longer and longer periods in the place of divine stillness that exists just beyond the boundaries of our anger and is always waiting for us.

CHAPTER 17
have your bags packed

"Then Mary said 'Here am I, servant of the
Lord; let it be with me according to your
word.'"
–Luke 1: 38

THAT WINTER, AS ADVENT BEGAN, I lost the ability to
sleep. Unexpectedly, as the month of December rolled
around, I was struck by an uncharacteristic bought of
insomnia that lasted for three weeks straight. There was
no straightforward explanation; I was not unusually
overstressed, overcommitted, or over-caffeinated. I didn't
put two-and-two together until I read Caryll Houselander's
description of the season and remembered the last month
of my pregnancy with my daughter. Houselander writes,
"And so we begin a season of growth and expectation—a
time to secret ourselves with Mary and join our hearts
with hers, and to grow pregnant with God together."

Seven years before, when I entered the home stretch of my pregnancy—when my daughter was still just a flutter and bump against my overstretched skin—I was similarly struck by a long stretch of sleeplessness. Night after night, without any particular worry or discomfort, I would lie wide awake. Almost all night, every night.

My OB-GYN diagnosed it as a case of "profound insomnia." I remember staring at him with irritable disbelief, wanting to grab him by his white coat lapels and shout, "You've got to be kidding me! Is that the best you can do? Is that all they taught you in medical school?" Despite my petulant attitude, I learned that "profound insomnia" is not uncommon in late-stage pregnancy. The sleeplessness resolved a few days before labor began.

Maybe that's how it was again that Advent season. Perhaps I was struck by a case of wakefulness and watchfulness as I joined with Mary and grew pregnant with God with her. As I prayed about this possibility, I felt the truth of it. Maybe it was because my hunger for actual pregnancy had been so acute for so long, but as I entertained the question, the vision of being expectant with Christ filled me with an immediate truth and rightness.

Houselander writes, "While Christ remained hidden in Mary, his rest was a tremendous activity; he was making her into himself, making himself from her." He was fully mingling their bodies and spirits, as he formed himself out of her flesh. This unfolded without any struggle or effort on her part, just a great waiting. As I meditated on this, I could almost feel Jesus reach out to touch my belly, sense his Spirit entering me. And with this, the stirrings of new life were somehow mysteriously within, ready to take shape in some unknown and unexpected form. I, too, was waiting.

I wanted to manifest this newfound sense of being pregnant with God in an embodied form. I felt an impulse to start waddling around like an eight-month pregnant lady. For one thing, I wanted a visible and outer signal to the world that it was time for me to slow down. I wanted the stream of emails at work to turn to a trickle as people around me started to anticipate a new beginning. God is coming and we need to rest, get the house ready, stock the freezer. Our bags have to be packed. We have to be on the lookout so that when the labor pains begin, we are ready to shed our old ways and embrace a newly transformed and up-ended life. And it will likely hurt. In John's gospel, Jesus uses the metaphor of pregnancy to warn and reassure us, "When a woman is in labor, she has pain, because her hour has come. But when her child is born, she no longer remembers the anguish because of the joy of having brought a human being into the world. So you have pain now; but I will see you again, and your hearts will rejoice and no one will take your joy from you." (John 16:16)

Yes, we grow pregnant with God together, and like any woman in the final trimester, we realize that birth will happen whether we are fully prepared or not. We have to be ready to discover the ways that God will show up in us and through us. And so for me, I couldn't sleep. And I couldn't wait to see what would happen next.

KATE H. RADEMACHER

PART 5

learning to rest and return

CHAPTER 18
there all along

"Most people know the sheer wonder that
goes with falling in love, how not only does
everything in heaven and earth become new,
but the lover himself becomes new."
–Caryll Houselander, *The Reed of God*

CHRISTMAS MORNING THAT YEAR felt different than any
before. I sat with my family as we opened gifts—box
after box containing Lego sets, watches, soaps, sweaters,
battery-operated dog robots. It was a familiar routine, but
at the edges of my consciousness, I could feel something
new. I retreated to the kitchen to fix a pan of scrambled
eggs and closed my eyes, leaning against the sink. Standing
there, in a brief moment of prayer, I could feel the Christ
child's presence. In my mind's eye, I could see him as an
infant in arms, imagined cradling him as Mary must have.

Lying skin to skin, gazing at his face—vulnerable, wrinkly, squirming and blinking in the unaccustomed light.

Pondering this image, aware of the newness of my Christian faith, I found the question pulsing in me: Did God *really* come to us on earth, embodied as a human son? In response, I could feel that yes, God really did come in the smallest, most vulnerable, ordinary thing of all: A human newborn.

The implications of this were shocking in their enormity.

For me, on that day—surrounded by the Christmas morning detritus of crumpled wrapping paper and boxes—I felt a huge, life-altering wonder, similar to a fleeting experience I'd had just after Lila had been born. It was a feeling that I'd been hungering to experience again ever since.

* * *

Over the years, as more and more friends have had children, I witnessed time and again the uniquely demoralizing and disorienting effects that postpartum depression can have. I've seen how it can sneak up unnoticed, feeding on the exhaustion and uncertainty of new motherhood, cruelly stripping the most accomplished, loving, and competent women of their confidence and equilibrium.

I do not know why or how I was spared this affliction when so many loved ones were leveled by it. I had numerous risk factors that made me vulnerable: a history of clinical anxiety, a pregnancy filled with medical challenges and emotional ambivalence. But for whatever reason, I had an entirely different postpartum experience: I was overcome with a profound and persistent euphoria after Lila's birth. It lasted in its most intense form for several weeks and lingered on in a milder version for months.

The overwhelming euphoria was connection, newfound perspective, and adoration. As a person who dwells too often in the mind, I loved having a job that was so fundamentally physical. The skin-on-skin contact, the carrying and cradling, the gazing at newborn eyes, toes, tongue, cheeks. It was a quieting of the mind, a silencing of the mental chatter and preoccupations that form the normal backdrop of my life.

My pregnancy had been plagued with uncertainty about whether I was ready to have a child; my timeline on the path to motherhood had been accelerated because of the age difference with David. My friends were all solidly oriented toward building their careers before they started families, and I was self-conscious to be the first among my peers to have a baby. A few weeks before the birth, I confessed to a friend that I was worried that motherhood was coming too soon for me. I was terrified that I would hate it and feel trapped.

I had read somewhere that every pregnancy and childbirth contains a question that must be answered. The question that plagued me was, "Am I ready?" And so, the relief was huge when I put my hand on my daughter's slippery skin just moments after she was born and felt the answer as a resounding "Yes." The relief made the adoration I felt for her even sweeter.

Yet the euphoria faded as the challenges of toddlerhood set in. And like the most desperate drug addict out there, I'd been craving another hit of the good stuff ever since then. This longing was at the heart of why I had dragged David and our marriage though so many endless, painful negotiations about whether to have another baby. Throughout all the years of struggle, my desire to experience that altered state of early motherhood again was insatiable.

At least, until that Christmas. After all the gifts were put away and the holiday meal consumed, I retreated upstairs. Turning back to prayer, I felt again a sense of Christ's arrival as a child for the world. In my imagination, vividly, he was an infant in my arms.

One of the reasons I experienced postpartum euphoria after my daughter's arrival was because, as the mother of a newborn, I had permission from my community to rest. Full cultural and internal permission for the first time—and the only time since—to step off the obsessive treadmill of activity and just be. That Christmas evening, I felt that same rare opportunity. An invitation to be with the Christ child—an invitation to become still, to observe, to connect. Compulsive productivity and awe-filled wonder don't go together. You have to give up one to allow the other in.

That Christmas, what I observed in the stillness was a change. I felt overcome with that almost drug-like wonder, connection, and awe as I allowed myself to dwell with the presence of the divine infant.

I was shocked. I hadn't realized that what I'd been yearning for had been there all along. I hadn't known that it had been there, in this way, the entire time.

CHAPTER 19

sabbath year

"For six years you shall sow your land and gather in its yield; but the seventh year you shall let it rest and lie fallow."

–Exodus 23: 10-11

WHEN I WENT BACK to work the week after New Year's that year, I felt almost as though someone had died. Practically everyone I know experiences some form of post-holiday blues. But that January, the sadness I felt was bigger and more persistent. For weeks, in the middle of meetings and everyday interactions, I found myself fighting back tears.

I realized I was grieving the plunge back into the anxiety and exhaustion of being overworked. Too often, the pace I maintain in order to meet the avalanche of deadlines, keep all the balls in the air and get all (or most) of the emails answered, means I'm left panting on the inside.

I kept recalling my Christmastime lesson: Compulsive productivity doesn't leave room for awe or wonder.

I had put up my Christmas tree early that year—just a few days after Thanksgiving—because I somehow thought it would serve as a permission slip to slow down. I waited all of December, but finally, late in the month, it happened. A spaciousness emerged in the holiday schedule, a rhythm of rest and delight. For ten days, I was able to do what my heart and the Spirit seemed to call for, hour by hour. No wonder I was grieving now that the nine-to-five routine had resumed and the To-Do list awaited at all times.

The antidote to compulsive productivity seems to be Sabbath-like rest. So how do you keep the borders of the Sabbath from being limited to one day a week?

Wayne Mueller's book *Sabbath* offers an interesting idea. He reminds us that, "The Hebrew practice of Sabbath included honoring the Sabbath year, when people refrained from planting, sowing seed, or harvesting crops. During this fallow time—an entire year of rest—the community relied upon whatever grew in the fields of its own. This served as a dramatic reminder that it was not their work alone, but rather God and the earth who fed them."

Perhaps this would be a Sabbath year for me. It had been seven years since Lila was born—seven years since I took a maternity leave and felt a deep permission from my community of coworkers and friends to go inward to honor and nurture the preciousness of new life. Seven years is a long time, especially because I felt as though my body and psyche had been clenched with effort that whole time. I'd been like a football player who has his shoulder shoved against a dummy mannequin during practice—pushing slowly inch-by-inch to make headway down the field. At work, I'd been trying to recover from being on the "Mommy Track," after I intentionally took a step down professionally when Lila was born so that I could work part-time. I felt like I had finally caught up from that "set back"—symbolically at least, when I had recently received a promotion at work. Even in my spiritual life, while all of my efforts to understand where God wanted me to head next had felt like holy work, the process had been laced with an element of striving. I'd been working hard—professionally, emotionally, spiritually—to grow and advance down the field of my life.

But perhaps now it was time to let the field lie fallow. What strikes me is that during the Sabbath year, things will still grow. What is different is that Sabbath time is all about what emerges on its own. It is not the square peg that I try to force through a round hole, but what appears organically, quietly, of God's original intention. The Sabbath year is an invitation to stop trying to push my agenda and instead get quiet so that God's agenda can emerge. As Mueller points out, it is a reminder that it is not my restless anxiety or effort alone that will feed me and the world, but God's generosity and grace. Perhaps this is what I can carry into my everyday interactions: An intention to avoid frantic striving and instead to sit back on my haunches and assume a position of inner repose, to see what springs forth on its own from this life God has provided.

A friend recently asked me about my regular, weekly Sabbath practice. "I understand what you don't do on the Sabbath. But what *do* you do?" My answer was "Nothing. And then I see what happens." On the prescribed day of rest, I've been able to embrace this discipline and have been surprised and delighted by the results. When I don't have any preset agenda, the day can unfold on its own. Sometimes this means dozing off on the couch in the afternoon, an unread book open on my chest. Or it means saying "yes" to Lila when she asks if we can get the Halloween make-up out and paint each other's faces or make a not-to-scale map of our neighborhood and then follow the map to see where it leads.

When I can stop multi-tasking and looking for the next thing to check off the list, rich interactions with others and moments of awareness and gratitude emerge. But I wondered, how could I carry this type of intention forward into the other days of the week and let it infuse the rhythm of regular life?

I visited my parents in Boston later that January. When we were out one afternoon, I passed by a young man working for Oxfam. With a friendly greeting, he asked if I wanted to give money to help put an end to famine. I shook my head, shoulders hunched, hurrying past. I proceeded over the next forty-five minutes to spend almost two hundred dollars on clothes. I later felt overcome with guilt and texted my brother, "Geez, what kind of Christian *am* I?" Guilt is no fun and is not a spiritual necessity, but I took my guilty feelings as a serious signal to ask the question: What would a Spirit-filled response have been in that moment? I realized that the huge deficit in my life is time. When I visited the same corner of the city as a high school and college student, money was tight, and I searched vigilantly for deals to make every cent count. But now the scarcity I feel in my life is a lack of time; my life is a rush to get everything done. I rarely go shopping and only had an hour that afternoon. I wanted to whip through four stores as quickly as possible. So I didn't stop to speak to the smiling volunteer, to ask him about his efforts, to perhaps donate some cash. I have worked for enough non-profit organizations to realize that very little of my money would have gone directly to help victims of famine. There was rent to pay for their Boston office, salaries for the fundraising staff, money for the pamphlets. But even so, the guy had a broad smile, and I wish I had stopped to chat, to thank him for his work. To pause for a beat and silently ask God, "How would you like me to respond in this moment, to this invitation? What is your will for me in this interaction?"

In his classic work *The Sabbath*, Abraham Joshua Heschel writes, "The Sabbath itself is a sanctuary which we build, a sanctuary in time." In our regular lives, time "is a measuring device rather than a realm in which we abide." Reclaiming the realm of time allows us to realize that "the goal is not to have but to be, not to own but to give, not to control but to share, not to subdue but to be in accord." By rushing past the Oxfam worker, I had just enough time to buy a sweater that, it turns out, is almost unbearably itchy, and a pair of pants that the Gap (perhaps rightly) claims are the "perfect trousers." But I missed a chance to delight in the moment, to soak up the Boston neighborhood I rarely visit anymore, a chance to smile and talk with a stranger who invited me to step out of compulsivity into a bigger relationship with my far-away neighbor who suffers today from devastating hunger.

My father accepted an invitation in his life to slow way down and, in doing so, entered into new and unexpected relationships. My dad was fortunate enough to be able to retire early. The vast majority of us will never have this luxury, and my father is certainly privileged. He also made a choice. He could have kept going in an effort to amass more wealth, fearful that his abundance would evaporate into scarcity. Instead, he stepped off that track. And his new schedule in retirement allowed him, one autumn afternoon, to take a walk with a neighbor and to have a conversation that would change both of their lives forever.

On their walk, the neighbor described his desperate worry about his adult son who had been born with bad kidneys. The son had already received two kidney transplants that had failed, and he was not doing well on dialysis. Listening to a mysterious, Spirit-filled nudge, my father went home, prayed, and a few days later volunteered to donate one of his own kidneys. He somehow felt this was what God wanted him to do. In the spaces that had emerged in his life, he was able to discern this as a calling.

Three years after the surgery, the transplant was a success. My father's health was good, the neighbor's son was stable and off of dialysis. But there was an even bigger surprise. About two years after the surgery, the wife of the kidney recipient got pregnant, and she gave birth to twin boys. Having kids had never been a realistic possibility for this family because of the husband's ongoing health crises. But all went smoothly, and the family was healthy and happy. We met the boys when they were just a few months old. They were beyond exquisite. Their dark eyelashes were lace on porcelain skin. Wrapped tightly in a fleece snuggie, one slept in my arms, while my mother cradled the other. Two lives that simply would not have existed if the pace of my father's life had not slowed down so that he could say "Yes" when God called.

I, like most others, am not in a position to take a year off of work to explore what a Sabbath year could mean in its fullest. But still, I wonder, how could I let the spirit of a Sabbath year play out in my life and infuse my path in the coming months? Could I, too, change the pace of my life even as I continued to work and parent? Could I remember that, as the *Book of Common Prayer* tells us, in "returning and rest we shall be saved"?

To start, I could remember that it takes awhile for natural growth to return. It requires patience to wait and see what the fields will yield if we're not poking and prodding them to produce according to our agenda. We must let the unfolding occur at its own pace.

I must also remember that this process can be uncomfortable. For instance, after getting the promotion at work that I'd been pushing and working so hard for over several years, I wasn't sure what would replace the relentless striving and low-grade anxiety that had become constant companions over the past few effort-filled years. I honestly didn't know if I could tolerate a practice of giving up control, didn't know if I could face the scary truth of what might emerge if I slowed down the pace. If I let the fields lie fallow, it might mean eating wild greens for a year, instead of the broccoli and tomatoes that I'm used to planting in my life. Could I live with that?

I could feel that a Sabbath year is not just about delighting in a slower pace, but is also letting in space to feel the grief of what's missing in our lives at the deepest level. Letting that grief point the way to what we must let go of and allow to change—even if it's scary as hell. It's also about letting a crack of joy swell with the knowledge and trust that somehow God will ease that grief and rise to meet us in our pain. A Sabbath year is about making space for God's promises to be fulfilled in our lives, in very unique and personal ways. It's letting the wind sweep through the garage and attic, blowing out the cobwebs and urging us to clean out the clutter, so that new, empty spaces can be created.

The growth I am invited into during a Sabbath year does not mean shrugging with passivity at life's events, sighing

"Oh well, I guess it just wasn't meant to be." Rather, it is acknowledging a growing understanding in my heart of what I am yearning to become, with and through God's love. It is recognizing what God is calling out to bloom. I typically think of the Sabbath as the absence of work. "Do nothing and see what happens." But it is the "see what happens" that is key—seeing what grows out of the resting. As Mueller writes, "We can touch where there is already an opening, a readiness, a place of grace waiting to be born."

Embracing a Sabbath perspective also teaches me about the nature of work. Work is not a dirty word. God does not exalt leisure over the important and necessary tasks that support our survival, the ways that we contribute and serve, the ways we most fully express our creativity. Instead, we can learn to approach and experience our work in a different way. Mueller writes "the ancient rabbis teach that on the seventh day, God created *menuha*— tranquility, serenity, peace and repose.... Until the Sabbath, creation was unfinished." Peace and serenity are essential ingredients of God's creation, which means that God doesn't intend for us to be doubled over with stress and straining. This is an essential re-learning for me, because our culture tells us that we should strive to do and be more, more, and more. I've internalized this message to such a degree that sometimes, ironically, when the pace slows down a little, I feel anxious in the absence of stress. Is something wrong? Am I missing something?

Disappointing someone? Or perhaps worst of all, will I be bored?

The former Archbishop of Canterbury, Rowan Williams, explores how we can approach our lives with greater balance in his book, *Where God Happens.* "We have to be strenuous yet relaxed," he writes. "We certainly know how to talk about being strenuous, how to portray Christian life as a struggle, a drama, in which we're called to heroic achievement and endurance, and we know how to talk about being relaxed, relying on God's mercy when we fail and not taking things too seriously. But it's far from easy to see how we can hold the two together. We can imagine the tightly strung pitch of effort, the slackness of relaxation: how are both possible at once?" He says that only "in the context of the common life" will we find the balance. The answer is not to step out of normal life into some sort of fantasyland of complete leisure, but to use the practice of living to seek and find that balance. It is like learning a martial art that calls for strength and power combined with a supple relaxation. I am far away from that ideal, but the potential of achieving that balance can be a good north star to guide me. And I don't have to turn the process into yet another self-improvement project to add to the list. Instead, I can set an intention during my Sabbath year to make adjustments to my workload and mentality in a relaxed, good-natured and non-hurried way.

One of the most painful things my father ever said to me was, "You can't have it all." I was six months postpartum and already champing at the bit for a bigger family and a bigger career to pay for it. My father's simple words felt like a betrayal—of the American dream, of the feminist mandate, and of the middle-class promise all at once. It was an insult to the implicit directive of my culture: Not only could I have it all, I practically had an obligation as a educated young woman with resources to seize all the unprecedented options in front of me. But I now understand the wisdom in my father's words. Every decision means that there's another choice that isn't made. Choosing rest on the Sabbath, for example, means giving up something else. There is a word for this: sacrifice.

I've wondered as I've tried to incorporate more of a Sabbath rhythm into everyday life whether the shift is about a change in quantity or quality. My gut and experience tell me it's both. It's not just about bringing a more tranquil mindset to my work. It's also about saying "no." Not just taking stuff off of my plate that I want to get rid of anyway, but also making tough choices and even hard sacrifices as part of a commitment to slow down and move closer to God. Jesus tells us that God "removes every branch in me that bears no fruit. Every branch that bears fruit he prunes to make it bear more fruit" (John 15:2-3). To slice off a branch that, at least superficially, appears to be healthy can be unnerving. Yet paradoxically, by allowing our lives to be pruned, the new growth that God envisions in us can flourish.

I realized that in this way my hunger for Sabbath was intimately connected to my hunger for another child.

When I became a mother, there were big changes in my life in terms of both quantity and quality of my activities. I cut the amount of my work way down. The quality of awe and wonder I experienced gave me perspective on what is truly important. I wanted both of those things back. In the weeks ahead, as I contemplated what the meaning of a Sabbath year might be, one of the first gifts I received was regaining some of that earlier perspective. I began feeling more grateful for all the things that were going right, not just clamoring to start the next project, gain the next insight, or position myself for the next accomplishment. And with all that was unresolved, all the decisions yet to be made, I felt more willingness to put my trust in God. Trust—often a radical trust—is the crucial ingredient when we ask how we can let go, give things up, risk disappointing others, cut down on compulsivity, be less productive. We are reminded by Jesus, "Do not keep striving for what you are to eat and what you are to drink, and do not keep worrying…. Instead, strive for his kingdom, and these things will be given to you as well" (Luke 22: 27-31).

I read recently that scientists aren't exactly sure why we evolved the need to sleep. Perhaps it is to forge new neural connections or to allow the brain to repair itself. The author described sleep and rest as providing "adaptive inactivity." This sounds about right. In a world filled with Tweets, tragedy, and unending tasks, inactivity *is* adaptive. We need a Sabbath practice—including perhaps an entire Sabbath year—to allow the frayed edges in the brain, body, and soul to be repaired. So, in the growing stillness, I prayed from the *Book of Common Prayer*:

"O Lord, support us all day long, until the shadows lengthen, and the evening comes, and the busy world is hushed, and the fever of life is over, and our work is done. Then in thy mercy, grant us safe lodging, and holy rest and peace at the last. Amen."

CHAPTER 20
heaven and earth

"Your kingdom come. Your will be done, on
earth as it is in heaven."
–Matthew 6:10

IN THE YEAR AFTER MY BAPTISM, a troubling question kept
coming back to me, over and over again. If Jesus had come
and set everything right, why wasn't the world *better*? Why
did the tragedy never end? Many of the losses that year
were unexpected and brutal. The young child of a close
friend died, and another friend was suddenly widowed
with two young children to raise. The daily newsfeed
was filled with stories about victims of school shootings,
refugees, terrorism, intractable poverty, civil war. Often,
I felt almost frantic in my grief for others. I tried to offer
support to friends and community members as best as I
could; I got involved with a few church ministries and

gave modest amounts of money away. But it all seemed profoundly, shamefully inadequate.

I had committed myself to the Christian path, but I still didn't fully know how to understand or respond to tragedy through a Christian lens. N.T. Wright writes that "something…happened in and through Jesus as a result of which the world is a different place." But *how* is it different? The more I got to know the members of the congregation at my new church, the more I realized how many people sitting in the pews beside me had suffered terrible losses or were struggling with substantial, ongoing challenges. For the most part, these people showed up week after week, composed, present. But I didn't want to be composed. I wanted to howl to the rafters. "How can life go on? Isn't there anything we can *do*?"

As Lent began that year, the golden, ornate cross that had been on display at church for several months was replaced with a statue of the crucified Jesus. One week, in a moment of self-awareness during the liturgy, I realized that I was averting my eyes from the statue. I didn't like to see Jesus on the cross: His body crumpled, collapsed, hanging. I felt much more comfortable with the resurrected Christ. I wanted the cross that was lavishly draped in white cloth after Easter. I was a new Christian, and the violent image of Christ's suffering left me cold.

My discomfort with Jesus' suffering somehow reminded me of my attitude toward the suffering around me. I yearned for redemption; I wanted to skip ahead to the collective happy ending. So I returned to the Jesus-infused version of the "Taking and Giving" prayer that had originally opened the door for me to know and experience Christ in my life. Each day, I imagined that Jesus was in me and that through him, I was breathing others' suffering into myself. In exchange, I imagined that I was breathing out God's peace to the world.

I found that this imaginative process of willingly taking on others' suffering slowly began to transform my perception—of myself and others. Jesus instructs us to love our neighbors as ourselves. Not to just love our neighbors, but to love them *as ourselves*. How do we most commonly manifest self-love? We cherish ourselves by trying to avoid—at all cost—anything that causes us discomfort and pain, whether that be the sting of everyday disappointments or the grief of bigger hurts. We contort ourselves every which way to get the job we want, the lover we desire, the belongings we covet, the health we feel we deserve, the baby we've longed for. But what if instead of wishing for all of this for ourselves, we were to cast that grasping aside and love others with the same ferocious intensity—seeking and praying that they become liberated from suffering and find true happiness and peace? What if, in fact, we were willing to take on all of the poison of their pain, and give them our own sweet and perhaps hard-won happiness?

The Buddhists describe the human experience as an "ocean of suffering." I'm sure if we consolidated all of the pain we've each felt, all of the horrible stories we've each heard, all of the anguish we've seen loved ones experience—if we combined all that, it would indeed fill up an ocean. I have spent countless hours contemplating this image, hungry to know what, if anything, can be done to find real solutions to human suffering.

On a trip to the beach over Lila's spring break that March, during an early morning prayer session one day, I brought this image to Jesus with a questioning heart. Sitting on the cool, sandy shore, I was graced with an understanding that yes, there is certainly an ocean of suffering. But at the same time, there is an ocean of joy, too. A huge, vast ocean of God's peace. These two realities exist together. It is as if heavenly and earthly experiences are two hands stacked on top of one another, fingers lightly interlaced. They are both entirely true, both simultaneously present.

In *Simply Christian*, N.T. Wright writes that "somehow, God's dimension and our dimension—heaven and earth—overlap and interlock...and will do so until creation is finally renewed and the two dimensions are joined into one as they were designed to be." This is the Christian promise; this is the Christian hope. In the meantime, "the Spirit is given to begin the work of making God's future real in the present." Wright continues, "those in whom the Spirit comes to dwell are to be the people who live at the intersection between heaven and earth."

We dwell at the intersection. Jesus created the bridge between heaven and earth, and now—when we allow ourselves to be guided by the Holy Spirit—we reside at the place where the two dimensions meet. It is an exciting thought, but I still often feel painfully inadequate as I try to respond to the rampant suffering that surrounds me.

That month at church, a beloved parishioner died. She had suffered from a serious, terminal illness, but we all thought she had longer to live, and the end came very suddenly. The last time I saw her, I had prayed with her, tried to offer reassurances and a bit of comfort. But my words felt clumsy and forced; I felt like I was trying to say something lofty and true and inspired, rather than letting the Spirit lead the way. Now it turned out I would never get another chance with this woman. After the church service that week, I stood beside the baptismal font, arms crossed, staring at the water. A friend approached, and I burst into tears. I explained my sense of inadequacy. She touched my shoulder and said, "Remember, we are only clay jars."

Yes, Saint Paul reminds us in his letter to the Corinthians that "we have this treasure in clay jars, so that it may be made clear that this extraordinary power belongs to God and not us" (2 Corinthians 4:7). We cannot heal the divide; we cannot knit heaven and earth together, although we desperately want to do so. Instead, we can stand at the intersection, feeling the wind of the Holy Spirit cross effortlessly between the ocean of suffering and the ocean of peace, feeling fully the existence of both realities. We take small steps forward as we discern how God is commissioning us to do God's work in the present, while at the same time each day we pray, "Your kingdom come. Your will be done, on earth as it is in heaven."

CHAPTER 21

all in

"Abide in me as I abide in you."
–John 15:4

In the community where I grew up, people generally reacted to Christianity as if they were touching a hot pan; they seemed to recoil automatically. In most of the circles I move in today, it's much the same. A month before the first anniversary of my baptism, I went out for lunch with two colleagues. Chatting over the meal, they joked about a mutual acquaintance who has a Jesus ringtone on his cell phone. I twitched uncomfortably in my seat, mostly because there was a big part of me that was thinking, "I have no idea what a Jesus ringtone is, but I want one, too!"

In moments like these, I found myself wondering: How did I get here? How does a liberal, Northern, intellectual, secular snob end up loving God with her whole heart?

Really the question is: How do any of us get lucky enough to be touched by God's immeasurable and extravagant grace? It comes, at least in my experience, by saying, "Yes," by opening one's heart to a nascent, undeniable connection. But even as my heart swelled with gratitude for the places that this connection has led, there are moments when I continue to feel anxiety and doubt—not about God's beauty or blessings, but about the cultural baggage that comes with Christianity. That day at lunch, I didn't defend our friend's ringtone choice. My colleagues didn't know anything about my conversion. I still hadn't told anyone at work, and only a handful of friends knew about my newfound religiosity.

The first essay I ever published about my spiritual life appeared in my church's monthly newsletter. Unbeknownst to me, they printed it along with a photo of me getting dunked by full immersion at my baptism during the Easter Vigil. My internal reaction at seeing the article was not what I had imagined it would be: A chance to modestly tuck my hair behind my ears while secretly enjoying seeing my words in print. Instead, at discovering the photo alongside the text, I flushed as the reality hit anew. "Dang girl, you're a Christian," I gulped. Describing my persistent, self-conscious anxiety to a friend, she said I reminded her of a gay person who needs to come out of the closet. David encouragingly told me that I needed to be "all in."

All in. What does this mean? An image comes to mind of Maria at the beginning of *The Sound of Music* who gave all of her clothes away to the poor so that she was left with only one sad looking sack of a dress. Being "all in," with brave, go-for-broke commitment is scary and, at the same time, holds tremendous allure.

As I took communion one day that month, imbibing Christ's body and blood, I asked for help. "Help me set aside my fears and self-consciousness," I silently requested. "Help me be 'all in.'" There at the altar, the words danced and spun in my mind. The words flipped, becoming, "In all." I realized in that moment that the process of ongoing conversion is not so much about me deciding whether I'm "in" or "out," but rather it is acknowledging and welcoming the reality that God, through Christ, is in all of us.

The writer Carl McColman describes in *The Big Book of Christian Mysticism* the inherent paradox in the belief that Christ was both human and divine. He writes, "Many critics of Christianity see this as some sort of two-tiered system that distinguishes between Christ and the lesser mortals." Indeed, a number of adults in my life growing up who were attracted to spirituality but who rejected Christianity felt that the premise of Jesus as God was somehow elitist. Why would God show up only in one person? Why can't God be in all of us? McColman goes on to write, "This criticism stems from a profound misunderstanding.... God poured the fullness of divinity into Mary's womb, and so Christ was born. Christ in turn, pours the fullness of his divinity into each and every Christian through the Holy Spirit.... The literal meaning of the word 'Christian' is 'little Christ.'" This means that Jesus is the "great bridge-builder" and that "we share not only his full humanity but also his full divinity." To be "all in," I realize, means to find and feel all the ways that Jesus and I abide in one another, to discover and witness the ways he abides in everyone.

For me, being "all in" also means being willing to give up the pick-and-choose approach to religion and commit to one path—a path that includes being challenged by ideas that flummox me. In the past, I was convinced of the benefits of a buffet approach to spirituality, seeing the value in selecting from the range of beautiful, truth-filled teachings that are out there in the world and leaving behind the lessons that seemed false or disturbing. Yet I have come to see that the problem with rejecting the unappealing lessons is that we can easily avoid being challenged. And if we do not expect our spiritual practice to challenge us—to rock us to the very core—that implies that nothing has to change, that we don't need to grow.

Being "all in," of course, is also about passionate engagement. Often children are our best teachers in this regard. During our annual spring trip to the beach, some family friends drove over to join us for the weekend. One of the adults took the kids out to a gigantic store full of beach kitsch. Each child was told they could spend a few dollars. They fanned out and began an intense relay of comparison shopping. Did they want the shark water pistol or the oversized seashell sunglasses? They picked up item after item, abandoning each in favor of another, more alluring choice. But Lila was different. She made a beeline for the key chain kiosk and, without pausing, plucked out an oversized, bright pink heart pendant with the words, "I love Jesus" in the middle. My friend who was chaperoning asked Lila if she was sure. Wouldn't she prefer a beach ball or a glow-in-the-dark fish aquarium? No, Lila was resolute. She wanted the pink "I love Jesus" key chain.

When they arrived back at the house and Lila happily displayed her new acquisition, my heart glowed with pride. Lila doesn't yet carry the heavy weight of cultural baggage that would lead her to wonder if perhaps such a trinket is tacky or worthy of ridicule. She observes adults in her life who have taken the plunge, risking commitment rather than staying on a pick-and-choose path. She sees adults who accept the demands and the hard-to-resolve challenges of religious life and who, in turn, experience the joy and richness that the disciplined spiritual path can offer. The emotional tenor she picks up on tells her that this is all a very, very good thing, and therefore she already has an easier time of opening her heart to the possibility of being "all in" than I do. Her new key chain proudly displayed on her belt loop is proof. But I'm catching up to her. Perhaps she and I will even get matching Jesus ringtones someday.

CHAPTER 22
still, you love me

"On hearing this, Jesus said to them, 'It is not
the healthy who need a doctor, but the sick.
I have not come to call the righteous, but
sinners.'"
–Mark 2:17

MY MOTHER CRIED when I became a Christian. A few
weeks before my baptism, we sat together over a morning
cup of coffee while tears rolled down her cheeks and
dripped onto her shirt, soaking the cloth. This wasn't what
she had planned or expected for me.

I realize this is not how it usually goes. One of my best
friends experienced a similar situation, but with one big
difference: Her mother cried because she was *leaving* the
church. Here was my mother crying as I prepared to
commit to a life of lovingly serving God and my neighbor.
What was wrong with this picture?

It was the same question my mother had asked herself decades earlier when she looked around her church when she was in her early twenties. What's wrong with this picture? It was the middle of the Civil Rights movement and the Vietnam War. Yet the church members around her seemed unmoved. In the affluent, entirely white congregation, there was no collective action to respond by standing up—visibly, bodily—for social justice and peace. My mother looked around and what she saw was apathy and inaction. Hypocrisy. Self-satisfaction. Smugness. My mother couldn't take it. She left with a feeling of betrayal, a feeling that lasted for over forty years.

After hearing this story, I had rolled the implicit question around in my head for months. It's a classic question, really: How do you embrace Christianity when so many Christians are, frankly, messed up? Most of my friends wouldn't even consider Christianity in their adulthood because they are dismayed by stories they read in the newspaper or memories from their childhood of Christians who were judgmental, sanctimonious, even cruel.

Yet Jesus reminds us that we don't send healthy people to a doctor. Likewise, he didn't come to minister to the pure and holy people. He knew what we all know—that each one of us falls short in countless ways. That is the whole point. The real question—the hard question—is how do we not become part of the problem? How do we avoid perpetuating a cycle of judgment and bitterness when we look at deeply troubling behaviors of other Christians?

How do we attempt to manifest Christ's kingdom now, embracing our difficult and disappointing neighbor with true and abiding love?

Once when I was seven years old, sitting in the backseat of our car, I asked my mother if she would still love me if I did bad things. What if I stole? Yes, she said, she would still love me. What if I killed someone and went to jail? Yes, she would be very sad, but she would still love me. I remember being shocked. Amazed. It was a defining moment, realizing that I was loved no matter what.

My mother cried that day during her visit before my baptism partly because she didn't understand. She didn't get how I could align myself with a group that had disappointed her so deeply. I wanted to explain it to her. In the subsequent weeks after she returned home, I tried out different, imagined conversations in my head with her. I finally figured out the question I had for her. In my internal conversation, I asked her, "Mom, what if, hypothetically, I was a selfish, jealous, indifferent jerk, and I told you I was going to church. Would you tell me I didn't belong there?"

I'm sure if I asked my mother that, she would respond similarly to how she replied when I was seven years old. Yes, she would say, of course you should go to church if you want. Even if you are being petty or jealous or unkind.

But Mom, I wanted to say, don't you see? The obvious truth is that I *am* those things. I am jealous and judgmental and selfish every day. I am indifferent to suffering and injustice so often, much too often. There are many times that I don't live up to my values, the values you tried to instill in me—values of generosity and justice. Yet clearly you still love me. And the love you feel for your daughter, the love I feel for my daughter—this gives us a glimmer, a taste, of how we can love our neighbors. Of what it would feel like to have a generous, embracing, unconditional love. Of how Christ loves us.

Do Christians fail to live up to our expectations? Do we all fail to live into the spiritual values we have been taught? Of course. But we can still love one another. This is our call. Our challenge. Our mandate. So, if I look around the pews of my own church or the pews of other churches I read about in the newspaper and I see something I don't like, I don't feel betrayed. I feel invited. Invited to change and transform myself, with God's help and grace. Jesus tells us outright that he has not come to call the righteous, but the sinners. So my mom shouldn't be surprised when the people at church are the ones who obviously need healing. We all do. And this is the very reason to commit to the spiritual path.

CHAPTER 23

devotion

> "If you believe, take the first step, it leads to
> Jesus Christ. If you don't believe, take the first
> step all the same, for you are bidden to take it.
> No one wants to know about your faith or your
> unbelief, your orders are to perform the act
> of obedience on the spot. Then you will find
> yourself in the situation where faith becomes
> possible and where faith exists in the true sense
> of the word."
>
> –Dietrick Bonhoeffer, *The Cost of Discipleship*

IN MY FIRST YEAR as a Christian, I experienced everything as shiny and brand new. The amount I didn't know about church history or Biblical interpretation could fill a silo. Yet everyday I felt like Charlie Bucket, the protagonist in Roald Dahl's *Charlie and the Chocolate Factory*. I wanted to sing out to the world, "I've got a golden ticket!" I was amazed to discover what was hidden from me in plain sight—that there is a whole other way of understanding the world and being in right relationship with it. The path involves eschewing the worldly concerns of praise, reputation, riches, comfort—and embracing a life of service and devotion.

William Law, the Anglican priest who wrote in the early 1700s, describes the "devout" as those people who "consider God in everything, serve God in everything, and make every aspect of their lives holy by doing everything in the name of God and in a way that conforms to God's glory." On one hand, this is a tall order. On the other hand, I feel like a schoolgirl bouncing in her seat, fingers stretched to the ceiling. "Ooo-ooo, pick me! Pick me! I want to sign up for that one!"

I was surprised by a letter I received from my former college chaplain which addressed the topic of devotion. In the staunchly secular academic environment of the small liberal arts college I attended, organized religion was not a big part of the scene. Yet the weekly, non-denominational Vespers offered by the chaplain was popular. A free dinner was served, which probably helped. We then gathered for a simple ritual, always diverse in orientation—ranging from silent meditation to recitation of poetry to singing and lighting of candles. I had gotten back in touch with the chaplain all these years later to thank him for Vespers, which had been an important part of my early spiritual formation, and to tell him about my conversion to Christianity. He wrote back celebrating the happy news.

He also shared the memory that he always observed me as being among "the most devout'" of students.

I was surprised by the word, *devout*. Surprised that even fifteen years ago—when I was more than a decade away from having a committed spiritual path—this was how the chaplain saw me. My identity since being baptized was that of convert, a neophyte just learning the A, B, Cs of what being a disciple of Christ means. Yet the chaplain's reflection helped me to see that this devotional orientation had been in me the whole time. Rather than involving a transformation into something totally new, the conversion journey was actually about becoming more of who I'd been all along.

Just as we try to follow the breadcrumbs that the Spirit leaves out to discern God's will for our actions in the outer world, we must seek to understand what our true identity is in God's eyes: Who we are, in the biggest sense. Who God means us to be.

My mother doesn't understand words like devotion; when I told her about the letter from my former chaplain, she crinkled her forehead. "What do you think he meant by that? Devout?" After a brief discussion, she changed the subject uncomfortably. In a classic mother-daughter dance, part of my journey to adulthood has been about individuation and understanding the ways that I am different from her.

My mother is an activist through-and-through. For more than fifteen years, she has fought against mandatory minimum sentencing for first-time, non-violent drug offenders, mainly men and women trapped in a cycle of poverty. When the group won a victory recently and some of the harshest sentencing laws in Massachusetts were changed to be more lenient, my mother reported, "It took over a decade of poking and prodding our state legislators on a regular basis. And a whole lot of patience." My mother remains uncomfortable with the idea of God, largely I think because she cares about justice so much. She can't stand a world that is full of so much unfairness; she can't believe that it is all part of God's plan.

Yet, I think this is a misunderstanding. God loves justice more than any of us. Marcus Borg addresses the uneasiness that my mother and so many others experience with common portrayals of God as the supernatural arbiter of events. He writes, "If God sometimes intervenes, how does one account for the nonintervention?.... If God could have intervened to stop the Holocaust but chose not to, what kind of sense does that make?.... To suppose that God intervenes implies that God does so for some, but not for others." In his book, *The Heart of Christianity*, Borg argues that a true understanding of the duality of God's transcendence and immanence means that "the notion of 'divine intervention' disappears in the precise sense" and instead "divine intention and divine interaction" are the essential elements of God's "presence beneath and within our everyday lives."

Divine intention. Divine interaction. Opening one's heart to experiencing both God's intention for us and God's interaction with us is what the path is all about.

God's intention is justice; scripture clearly points to this. The interaction comes in listening for, discerning, and heeding the ways that God calls us to help live into this vision for a just and perfect Kingdom. By following the red bird when it appears in our lives, we slowly, haltingly learn more and more of what God's divine intention is for us and discover the apex where, as Frederick Buechner describes, our "deep gladness and the world's deep hunger meet." For my mother, this takes the form of social activism; working for justice is her deepest gladness as she rises up to meet the world's needs. Although she would remain uneasy with this characterization, I think she is living out God's intention for her.

On his deathbed, my great-great-grandfather, the Rev. Robert South Barrett, wrote about the unexpected freedom that comes with devoting our lives to God's vision for us. In 1884, he was appointed as General Missioner of the Episcopal Church, a prestigious national position very different from his early commission in the tiny church in Richmond's slum community. For a little over a year, he crisscrossed the country, a popular preacher and theologian. Then, a few months later at age forty-five, he was diagnosed with a terminal illness. Within a year he died, leaving his wife and six young children. In his final months, he wrote a book of essays entitled *A Reason of the Hope*, published just before his death. Writing about the timeless paradox of devotion, he described two magnolia trees he'd seen when he was dean of the cathedral in Atlanta:

"We would think that when I give up my will to Christ that I give up my freedom. But as strange as it may seem, Faith liberates the soul…. In a Georgia city, I have seen two magnolia trees which were planted in the same year. One of them was tall and straight and symmetrical, the leaves were brilliantly green, the flowers gloriously fresh and white and fragrant. The other tree was dwarfed and bent and one-sided, its leaves were narrow and yellow, there was no bloom. The cause of this contrast was easy to see. One tree was standing alone in the square, with plenty of room and sunlight and air. The other was confined and shadowed by the houses, and its roots were cramped by the pavement. One was free and the other was not free. Free to do what? Free from law? On the contrary, the very reverse. One was free to follow its law; the other was not free to follow its law. Every created thing has a divine law, a divine plan, a divine ideal. When let alone and free to follow that law, that ideal, it reaches perfection. That tall, straight, succulent, blooming, fragrant Magnolia was free to follow its law; the other was not free."

Following the divine plan is about freely living out God's intention for us. This is why my conversion journey and my mother's fight for justice—while two different paths—have both been about becoming more of our true selves and embracing the divine spark that has burned in us the whole time.

As we seek and live out our unique path of devotion, we must remember the call to do everything "in a way that conforms to God's glory." On the night I finished the first draft of this book, I lay awake, tossing and turning, gripped with waves of doubt and self-condemnation. The fears swirled around: The first section was all wrong; the writing was amateurish and flabby; I was embarrassed to show anyone a first draft. At dawn, I got up and prayed for guidance. It was a week before Easter; it would be the first anniversary of my baptism. Turning to the Psalms, the words leapt out at me, "Not to us, O Lord, not to us, but to your Name give glory" (Psalm 115:1). I realized all the anxious self-critiquing was about ego; deep down, I wanted to fulfill a fantasy of my own greatness. Our habits of self-cherishing alternate between chasing after a vision of our excellence and running away from our fear of inadequacy. Both of these stances revolve around self-concern. Instead, I realized, my call was to press on, with a single-hearted desire to glorify God in whatever form God calls me to do this.

We must act with a heart of devotion, whether we are painting the Sistine Chapel or sweeping its floor. At the outset, we often don't know which one we've been assigned to do. We don't know whether the outcome will include worldly success and grandeur, or not. The scientist doesn't know if she will win the Nobel Prize or if the experiment will be a bust. The artist doesn't know if the painting will hang in a gallery or get stuck in a drawer. The parent doesn't know if he's raising a future Supreme Court justice or a high school dropout. It doesn't matter. We must do these things with love, with dedication, and with passion. Of course, the alluring temptations of praise and reputation remain. It is a hard discipline to renounce a desire for accolades. But even if our Spirit-filled acts have no hope of leading to any kind of popular success or recognition, the point is to maintain a heart of devotion as we respond to God's call. Even when the reason for the call is unclear and the outcome is, at best, uncertain.

That morning, as I rededicated my heart to acting for God's glory, not my own, my eyes lifted from the page. Outside the window, the tree branches traced a delicate silhouette in the sky. A cardinal with vivid red wings landed on the branch straight ahead of me. And so, with a commitment to follow, I take the next small, stumbling step forward.

ACKNOWLEDGEMENTS

THIS BOOK WOULD NOT have been written without the steadfast support, guidance, and encouragement of the Rev. Liz Dowling-Sendor. She has been the book's midwife, and I am hugely grateful for all of the ways she facilitated and delighted in the birthing of this book. I am also thankful for one of the best ministries Liz offered: lending me dozens and dozens of books, including many quoted here. The authors of these books have been my teachers and guides over the past four years and have shaped my formation as a new Christian in countless ways.

With gratitude to Erica Witsell who carefully reviewed multiple drafts of the manuscript. I am thankful for her insightful edits, and for her enthusiasm and support which buoyed me throughout this entire process.

With thanks to Laura MacCarald who was one of the first reviewers of the book, and whose lifelong friendship has been so precious to me. With thanks to Caroline Wells

Pence and Kat Tumlinson for walking with me through this journey in friendship and as compassionate listeners and loving witnesses. With gratitude to Steve Erickson for giving me the idea for the title of the book, and for being a spiritual friend for so many years. With thanks to Dana Trent for all of her support, help, and advice particularly in the final phase as I was completing the manuscript and seeking a publisher.

With immense gratitude to the Rev. Dr. Clarke French, the Rev. Sarah Ball-Damberg, and all of the other staff and parishioners at the Church of the Holy Family in Chapel Hill, North Carolina. It is incredible to have found a place that feels like such a true spiritual home, and I am thankful everyday that you are my holy family.

With thanks to the Rev. Maj-Britt Johnson who provided the container that allowed this journey to begin, and to the Rev. Wren Blessing for reading early drafts of many of these chapters. With gratitude to Peggy Payne for her support and skillful editing, and to the Rev. Gary Comstock for seeing the devotion in me all those years ago.

With special thanks to members of the Kosala Mahayana Buddhist Center in Carrboro, North Carolina for their support of me on this journey, and with tremendous gratitude for the kindness of the Geshe Kelsang Gyatso.

I am enormously grateful to the team at Light Messages Publishing for believing in this book and for all they have done to launch it into the world. With special thanks to Elizabeth Turnbull for her support, thoughtful edits, and the beautiful cover, and to Kylee Wooten for her advice and guidance.

I am incredibly thankful for the friends and family who have supported me in the conversion journey, patiently listened to me talk about the writing process, and provided invaluable feedback on early drafts of various sections of the book. With special thanks to John and Brittney Holbein, Krista Bremer and Ismail Suayah, Elsie Kagan, Trinity Zan, Tricia Petruney, Krista, Peter and Joshua Alexander, Laura Gallagher, Heather Vahdat, Bill Finger, Karen Stegman and Alyson Grine, Meredith Leight, Dave Worster, Carol McGuire, Mia Lipman Irwin, Kirsten Krueger, Rebecca Callahan, Lucy Wilson, Jill Sergison, Barbara Lorie, Stacye Leanza, Clara MacCarald, Pam Rademacher, Kristen Rademacher, Angela Conant, Eva Lyman-Munt, and Tina MacDonald.

Most of all, with unending gratitude to Bruce and Lynn Holbein who are the best parents anyone could ever hope to have. They have inspired me and cheered me on in countless ways, too many to name. I am grateful beyond measure for my mother's authenticity, tough questions, humor, commitment to justice, and loving friendship. I am thankful for my father's quiet and unimposing invitation to check out the path, for his love and remarkable generosity, and for the example he provides. I am grateful everyday for my wonderful brothers, Chris and Andrew, for their amazing friendship and for all of the ways that they encourage me, hold me up, and inspire me.

And with enormous gratitude to Soren and Lila for being such amazing kids and for their patience and support during this process. And to David, my best friend, for his love and for all the ways he has modeled the spiritual path and offered me the space to grow more and more into my true self.

NOTES

All Scripture quotations, unless otherwise indicated, are taking from the Holy Bible, New Revised Standard Version. Scripture quotations marked "KJV" are taken from the Holy Bible, King James Version.

Epigraph

Lewis, C. S. *The Lion, the Witch and the Wardrobe*. 1950. New York: HarperTrophy, 1994.

Introduction

Luhrmann, T. M. *When God Talks Back: Understanding the American Evangelical Relationship with God*. New York: Alfred A. Knopf, 2012.

Chapter 1

Gilbert, Elizabeth. *Eat, Pray, Love: One Woman's Search for Everything Across Italy, India and Indonesia*. New York: Penguin Books, 2006.

Luhrmann, T. M. *When God Talks Back: Understanding the American Evangelical Relationship with God*. New York: Alfred A. Knopf, 2012.

Chapter 2

Lewis, C. S. *Mere Christianity: A Revised and Amplified Edition, with a New Introduction, of the Three Books, Broadcast Talks, Christian Behaviour, and Beyond*

Personality. 1952. San Francisco: HarperSanFrancisco, 2001.

Chapter 4

Borg, Marcus J. *Meeting Jesus Again for the First Time: The Historical Jesus and the Heart of Contemporary Faith.* New York: HarperOne, 1994.

Episcopal Church. *The Book of Common Prayer and Administration of the Sacraments and Other Rites and Ceremonies of the Church.* New York: Oxford University Press, 2007.

Lewis, C. S. *Mere Christianity: A Revised and Amplified Edition, with a New Introduction, of the Three Books, Broadcast Talks, Christian Behaviour, and Beyond Personality.* 1952. San Francisco: HarperSanFrancisco, 2001.

Norris, Kathleen. *Amazing Grace: A Vocabulary of Faith.* New York: Riverhead Books, 1998.

O'Driscoll, Henry. *Emmanuel: Encountering Jesus as Lord.* Cambridge: Cowley Publications, 1992.

Wolfe, Gregory. *The New Religious Humanists* as quoted in Norris, Kathleen. *Amazing Grace: A Vocabulary of Faith.* New York: Riverhead Books, 1998.

Chapter 5

Lewis, C. S. M*ere Christianity: A Revised and Amplified Edition, with a New Introduction, of the Three Books,*

Broadcast Talks, Christian Behaviour, and Beyond Personality. 1952. San Francisco: HarperSanFrancisco, 2001.

Luhrmann, T. M. *When God Talks Back: Understanding the American Evangelical Relationship with God.* New York: Alfred A. Knopf, 2012.

Merton, Thomas. *New Seeds of Contemplation.* 1972. New York: New Directions Books, 2007.

Taylor, Barbara Brown. *The Preaching Life.* Cambridge: Cowley Publications, 1993.

Teresa, Mother. *Where There is Love, There is God: A Path to Closer Union with God and Greater Love for Others.* New York: Image, 2010.

Chapter 6

Palmer, Parker J. *Let Your Life Speak: Listening for the Voice of Vocation.* San Francisco: Jossey-Bass, 2000.

Chapter 7

Merton, Thomas. *New Seeds of Contemplation.* 1972. New York: New Directions Books, 2007.

Palmer, Parker J. *Let Your Life Speak: Listening for the Voice of Vocation.* San Francisco: Jossey-Bass, 2000.

Taylor, Barbara Brown. *The Preaching Life,* Cambridge: Cowley Publications, 1993.

Wells, Samuel. *What Episcopalians Believe: An Introduction.* New York: Morehead Publishing, 2011.

Chapter 8

Barrett, Kate Waller. "Some Reminiscences." *The Florence Crittenton Magazine.* March, 1899.

Luhrmann, T. M. *When God Talks Back: Understanding the American Evangelical Relationship with God.* New York: Alfred A. Knopf, 2012.

Norris, Kathleen. *Amazing Grace: A Vocabulary of Faith.* New York: Riverhead Books, 1998.

Westerhoff, John H. with Pearson, Sharon Ely. *A People Called Episcopalians: A Brief Introduction to Our Way of Life.* 2002. New York: Morehouse Publishing, 2014.

Chapter 9

Episcopal Church. *The Book of Common Prayer and Administration of the Sacraments and Other Rites and Ceremonies of the Church.* New York: Oxford University Press, 2007.

Guenther, M. *The Practice of Prayer.* Lanham: A Cowley Publications Book, 1998.

Lewis, C. S. *The Screwtape Letters.* London: Geoffrey Bles, 1942.

Chapter 11

Guenther, M. *The Practice of Prayer.* Lanham: A Cowley Publications Book, 1998.

Chapter 12

Nouwen, Henri J.M. *In the Name of Jesus: Reflections on Christian Leadership.* New York: The Crossroad Publishing Company, 1989.

Waldron R. *Poetry as Prayer: The Hound of Heaven.* Boston: Pauline Books & Media, 1999.

Chapter 13

Kempis, Thomas a, *The Inner Life. An excerpt from The Imitation of Christ.* New York: Penguin Books, 2005.

Chapter 14

Merton, Thomas. *New Seeds of Contemplation.* 1972. New York: New Directions Books, 2007.

Sendak, Maurice. *Where the Wild Things Are.* New York: Harper & Row, 1963.

Chapter 15

Holmes, Urban T. III and John H. Westerhoff III. *Christian Believing.* New York: The Seabury Press, Inc, 1979.

Chapter 17

Hoffman, Thomas, ed. *A Child in Winter: Advent, Christmas, and Epiphany with Caryll Houselander.* Franklin: Sheed & Ward, 2000.

Chapter 18

Houselander, Caryll. *The Reed of God.* New York: Sheed & Ward, 1944.

Chapter 19

Episcopal Church. *The Book of Common Prayer and Administration of the Sacraments and Other Rites and Ceremonies of the Church.* New York: Oxford University Press, 2007.

French, Christopher. "Why Did Sleep Evolve?" *Scientific American.* January/February, 2013.

Heschel, Abraham Joshua. *The Sabbath.* 1951. New York: Farrar, Staus and Giroux, 1979.

Muller, Wayne. *Sabbath: Finding Rest Renewal, and Delight in our Busy Lives.* New York: Bantam Books, 1999.

Williams, Rowan. *Where God Happens: Discovering Christ in One Another.* Boston: New Seeds, 2005.

Chapter 20

Wright, N.T. *Simply Christian: Why Christianity Makes Sense.* New York: HarperOne, 2006.

Chapter 21

McColman, Carl. *The Big Book of Christian Mysticism: The Essential Guide to Contemplative Spirituality.* Charlottesville, VA: Hampton Roads Pub., 2010.

Chapter 23

Barrett, Robert South. *A Reason of the Hope.* Washington D.C.: National Publishing Company, 1896.

Bonhoeffer, Dietrich. *The Cost of Discipleship.* 1937. New York: Macmillian Publishing Co., 1961.

Borg, Marcus J. *The Heart of Christianity: Rediscovering a Life of Faith.* New York: Harper Collins, 2003.

Buechner, Frederick. *Wishful Thinking: A Seeker's ABC.* San Francisco: HarperSanFrancisco, 1993.

Law, William. *A Serious Call to a Devout and Holy Life* as quoted in Foster, Richard J. and Smith James, *Devotional Classics: Selected Readings for Individuals and Groups.* New York: HarperOne, 1989.

ABOUT THE AUTHOR

KATE RADEMACHER grew up outside of Boston and now lives in Chapel Hill, North Carolina with her family. She works in international public health, and in her writing, she explores the ways that we can listen for and respond to God's call. She is currently working on her second book about her experience as a foster parent. Connect with Kate online at katerademacher.com.

If you liked

FOLLOWING THE RED BIRD

you might also enjoy these titles from
Light Messages Publishing & Torchflame Books

Faith and Air: The Miracle List
Scott Mason
Coming Fall 2017

Raised by Strangers
Brooke Lynn

From Fortress to Freedom
Deborah L.W. Roszel

Jonah: A Tale of Mercy
Jimmy Long